FROM THE

LIBRARY OF

ROBERT
VARNAM

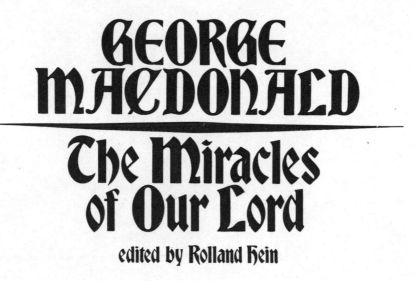

GEORGE MACDONALD

The Miracles of Our Lord

edited by Rolland Hein

Harold Shaw Publishers
Wheaton, Illinois

THE MIRACLES OF OUR LORD *first published in 1871.*

Library of Congress Cataloging in Publication Data
Macdonald, George, 1824-1905.
  The miracles of our Lord.

  Includes index.
    1. Jesus Christ—Miracles.   *I. Hein, Rolland.*
II. Title.
BT366.M29   1980   232.9'5   79-22261
ISBN 0-87788-547-8

Printed in the United States of America

CONTENTS

FOREWORD

We live in the midst of a miracle. The physical world around us, ever-changing in its mystery and beauty, is "the great and I suspect the only miracle," MacDonald writes. It is this same miracle of creation which we see at work in the miracles of Jesus Christ — wonders which differ from the "great" miracle only in the speed in which they were accomplished. In the miracles of our Lord, God's power was manifested suddenly and dramatically, while in our everyday world this same power works quietly. Today, God continues to heal the sick, calm nature's storms, and multiply our harvests; however, people's senses, dulled by the ordinary, fail to understand these "common-place" events and processes as miraculous.

In this work, MacDonald does not make any attempt to give an allegorical interpretation of the miracles of Christ. Nor does he try to offer a theological defense of the probability of miracles — although he firmly defends their reality. "Happy are they who demand a good reason and yet can believe a wonder," he remarks. Rather, MacDonald's main concern is to consider these events in the life of our Lord in order to discover what they reveal about the nature of God the Father, and His relationship to man through Christ.

In his personal life, MacDonald sought to know the God who perfectly satisfied Jesus Christ. From the miracles of Christ, Mac-Donald learned more of Christ's knowledge of His Father, and how this knowledge helped Christ respond in obedience to the Father's will. MacDonald, in turn, shares these insights with us. For example, writing on St. John's account of the healing of the man blind from birth, MacDonald observes:

> *What a divine invention, what a mighty gift of God, is this very common thing —these eyes to see with —that light which enlightens the world, this sight which is the result of both. What a believer the man born blind must have become! Nothing should be too grand and good for him to believe thereafter —not even the doctrine hardest to common-place humanity, though the most natural and reasonable to those who have beheld it —that the God of the light is a faithful, loving, upright, honest, and self-denying being, utterly devoted to the uttermost good of those whom He has made.*

The miracle of his healed sight helped the once-blind man to understand the goodness of God in a totally new way. For perhaps the first time in his life, he was aware of God's loving goodness at work in nature. This same goodness, MacDonald teaches, is freely available to all men—it is only necessary for man to claim it.

Too often, however, man does not understand God's goodness because man is not good. God's purpose is to perfect man, and everything He does has a part in this plan. Because of this, Mac-Donald believes that all of man's problems and difficulties are necessary to help man become more Christ-like. This does not mean that such sufferings are "good," but rather that they may bring about good results. Christ's miracles, in relieving some men's miseries, were also a part of God's plan to effect good. However, it must be remembered that Christ did not heal all sick men, but only those whose illness had already begun to work positive results in their lives. These men were able to learn from their miraculous cures, and with this knowledge, enter into a firmer spiritual relationship with God.

MacDonald's belief in the necessity of human suffering does not mean that he minimizes the problem of evil in our world. Certainly it is never easy to understand why God has chosen to work in men's lives through pain, which is a result of the evil. However, MacDonald believes that the answer to this question may be found when an individual willingly accepts *all* the experiences in his life—both the good and the bad. God rewards such child-like faith by helping man in his efforts in the "unravelling ... of the knotted and twisted coil of the universe." Man must be confident in the ultimate rightness of God's actions, and have faith that someday he will receive the knowledge necessary to give him true understanding of God's ultimate purpose.

The objection may be raised that George MacDonald lived in the morally clear-cut and more comfortable world of the Victorians, and no matter how interesting his ideas may be, they are too naive, inadequate for our complex and corrupt twentieth century. However, before making such a hasty judgment, one would be wise to examine MacDonald's own life and the awesome personal suffering which he endured—remembering also, that his deeply held convictions arise from this life-context.

The realities of poverty, sickness, and the frequent death of loved ones were a part of MacDonald's life. As a child, he suffered many hardships on his father's farm, near Huntly, Scotland, where he was born in 1824. He lost his mother when he was eight, and was often ill as a child. As a young pastor in the early 1850's, he knew the frustrations and discouragements of trying to minister to an antagonistic congregation—so antagonistic, in fact, that they reduced his already inadequate salary in order to force him to leave. With a growing family, a compelling sense of call to the Lord's work, and a desire to be a writer, MacDonald eked out a living for years, accepting the help of friends and a few sympathetic supporters. Finding enough money just to buy groceries was for a prolonged period an almost daily worry.

But this wasn't all. MacDonald's own health was poor, and he experienced recurring attacks of profuse hemorrhaging from the lungs, pleurisy, eczema, chronic indigestion, bronchitis, and asthma. But perhaps the deepest of all pain was the loss of four of his children. His biographer son writes of his father's grief at the death of Lilia, his eldest daughter, in 1891: "Her father could hardly leave the grave: he came back twice after all others had left, and it was with difficulty he was at last led away."* To be sure, Lilia's death occurred after the publication of *The Miracles of our Lord* (1871), but MacDonald's attitudes toward adversity and death were constant throughout his life. His firm confidence that all such events are the raw materials of God's creative purpose is well summarized in his book-length calendar poem, *The Diary of an Old Soul:*

> *Creation thou dost work by faint degrees,*
> *By shade and shadow from unseen beginning;*
> *Far, far apart, in unthought mysteries*
> *Of thy own dark, unfathomable seas,*
> *Thou will'st thy will . . . .*

> *Well mayst thou then work on indocile hearts*
> *By small successes, disappointments small;*
> *By nature, weather, failure, or sore fall;*
> *By shame, anxiety, bitterness, and smarts;*
> *By loneliness, by weary loss of zest:*
> *The rags, the husks, the swine, the hunger-quest,*
> *Drive home the wanderer to the Father's breast! (July 10, 11)*

In this volume of meditations on the miracles of Christ, George MacDonald gives us insights into the uses which God can make of adversities, whether we are immediately delivered from such circumstances or not.

Please note that I have somewhat condensed the original text, removing repetitious material and ornate figures of speech. I have as well added headings and Scripture references, and have changed Biblical quotations from the King James Version to the Revised Standard. The questions for thought and discussion are also mine.

Rolland Hein
January 1979

---

*Greville MacDonald, *George MacDonald and His Wife,* London, George Allen & Unwin, 1924, p. 526.

ONE
INTRODUCTION

I have been requested to write some papers on our Lord's miracles. I venture the attempt in the belief that, seeing they are one of the modes in which His unseen life found expression, we are bound through them to arrive at some knowledge of that life. For He has come, The Word of God, that we may know God: every word of His then, as needful to the knowing of Himself, is needful to the knowing of God. And we must understand, as far as we may, every one of His words and every one of His actions, which, with Him, were only another form of word.

I believe this the immediate end of our creation. And I believe that this will at length result in the unravelling for us of what must now, more or less, appear to every man the knotted and twisted coil of the universe.

It seems to me that it needs no great power of faith to believe in the miracles — for true faith is a power, not a mere yielding. There are far harder things to believe than the miracles. For a man is not required to believe in them save as believing in Jesus. If a man can believe there is a God, he may well believe that, having made creatures capable of hungering and thirsting for Him, He must be capable of speaking a word to guide them in their feeling after Him. And if He is a grand God, a God worthy of being God, yes, if He is a God capable of being God, He will speak the clearest, grandest word of guidance intelligible to His creatures.

For us, that word must simply be the gathering of all the expressions of His visible works into an infinite human face, lighted up by an infinite human soul behind it, namely, that potential essence of man, if I may use a word of my own, which was in the beginning with God. If God should *thus* hear the cry of the noblest of His creatures, for such are all they who do cry after Him, and in very deed show them His face, it is but natural to expect that the deeds of the great messenger should be just the works of the Father done in little. If He came to reveal His Father in miniature, as it were (for in these unspeakable things we can but use figures, and the homeliest may be the holiest), to tone down His great voice, which, too loud for men to hear it aright, could but sound to them as an inarticulate thundering, into such a still small voice as might enter their human ears in welcome human speech, then the works that His Father does so widely, so grandly that they transcend the vision of men, the Son must do briefly and sharply before their very eyes.

This, I think, is the true nature of the miracles, an epitome of God's processes in nature beheld in immediate connection with their source — a source as yet lost to the eyes and too often to the hearts of men in the far-receding gradations of continous law. That men might see the will of God at work, Jesus did the works of His Father thus.

Here I will suppose some honest, and therefore honorable, reader objecting: But do you not thus place the miracles in dignity below the ordinary processes of nature? I answer: The miracles are mightier far than any goings on of nature as beheld by common eyes, dissociating them from a living Will; but the miracles are surely less than those mighty goings on of nature with God beheld at their heart. In the name of Him who delighted to say "My Father is greater than I," I will say that His miracles in bread and in wine were far less grand and less beautiful than the works of the Father they represented, in making the corn to grow in the valleys, and the grapes to drink the sunlight on the hillsides of the world, with all their infinitudes of tender gradation and delicate mystery of birth. But the Son of the Father be praised, who, as it were, condensed these mysteries before us, and let us see the precious gifts coming at once from gracious hands — hands that love could kiss and nails could wound.

There are some, I think, who would perhaps find it more possible to accept the New Testament story if the miracles did not stand in the way. But perhaps, again, it would be easier for them to accept both if they could once look into the true heart of these miracles. So long as they regard only the surface of them, they will, most likely, see in them only a violation of the laws of nature: when they behold the heart of them, they will recognize there at least a possible fulfillment of her deepest laws. With such, however, is not my main business now, any more than with those who cannot believe in a God at all, and therefore to whom a miracle is an absurdity.

I may, however, just make this one remark with respect to the latter — that perhaps it is better they should believe in no God than believe in such a God as they have yet been able to imagine. Perhaps thus they are nearer to a true faith — except indeed they prefer the notion of the Unconscious generating the Conscious, to that of a self-existent Love, creative in virtue of its being love. Such have never loved woman or child save after a fashion which has left them content that death should seize on the beloved and bear them back to the maternal dust. But I doubt if there can be any who thus would choose a sleep-walking Pan before a wakeful Father. At least, they cannot know the Father and choose the Pan.

Let us then recognize the works of the Father as epitomized in the miracles of the Son. What in the hands of the Father are the mighty motions and progresses and conquests of life, in the hands of the Son are miracles. I do not myself believe that He valued the working of these miracles as He valued the utterance of the truth in words. But all that He did had the one root, *obedience,* in which alone can any son be free. And what is the highest obedience? Simply a following of the Father—a doing of what the Father does. Every true father wills that his child should be as he is in his deepest love, in his highest hope. All that Jesus does is of His Father. What we see in the Son is of the Father. What His works mean concerning Him, they mean concerning the Father.

Much as I shrink from the notion of a formal shaping out of design in any great life, so unlike the endless freedom and spontaneity of nature (and He is the Nature of nature), I cannot help observing that His first miracle was one of creation—at least, is to our eyes more like creation than almost any other—for who can say that it was creation, not knowing in the least what creation is, or what was the process in this miracle?

TWO

THE BEGINNING OF MIRACLES

(John 2:1-11)

*A*lready Jesus had His disciples, although as yet He had done no mighty works. They followed Him for Himself and for His mighty words. With His mother they accompanied Him to a merry-making at a wedding. With no retiring regard, with no introverted look of self-consciousness or self-withdrawal, but more human than any of the company, He regarded their rejoicings with perfect sympathy, for whatever suffering might follow, none knew so well as He that—

"there is one
Who makes the joy the last in every song."

The assertion in the old legendary description of His person and habits, that He was never known to smile, I regard as an utter falsehood, for to me it is incredible—almost as a geometrical absurdity.

In that glad company the eyes of a divine artist, following
the spiritual lines of the group, would have soon settled on
His face as the center whence radiated all the gladness,
where, as I seem to see Him, He sat in the background beside His mother. Even the sunny face of the bridegroom
would appear less full of light than His. But something is at
hand which will change His mood. For no true man had He
been if His mood had never changed. His high, holy, obedient will, His tender, pure, strong heart never changed, but
His mood, His feeling did change. For the mood must
often, and in many cases ought to be the human reflex of
changing circumstance.

The change comes from His mother. She whispers to
Him that they have no more wine. The bridegroom's lib-
erality had reached the limit of his means, for, like his
guests, he was, most probably, of a humble calling, a crafts-
man, say, or a fisherman. It must have been a painful little
trial to him if he knew the fact; but I doubt if he heard of the
want before it was supplied.

There was nothing in this however to cause the change
in our Lord's mood of which I have spoken. It was no serious catastrophe, at least to Him, that the wine should fail.
His mother had but told Him the fact; only there is more
than words in every commonest speech that passes. It was
not His mother's words, but the tone and the look with
which they were interwoven, that wrought the change. She
knew that her son was no common man, and she believed in
Him, with an unripe, unfeatured faith.

This faith, working with her ignorance and her fancy, led
her to expect the great things of the world from Him. This
was a faith which must fail that it might grow. Imperfection
must fail that strength may come in its place. It is well for
the weak that their faith should fail them, for it may at the
moment be resting its wings upon the twig of some brittle
fancy, instead of on a branch of the tree of life.

But, again, what was it in His mother's look and tone that

should work the change in our Lord's mood? The request implied in her words could give Him no offence, for He granted that request; and He never would have done a thing He did not approve, should His very mother ask Him. The *thoughts* of the mother lay not in her words, but in the expression that accompanied them, and it was to those thoughts that our Lord replied. Hence His answer, which has little to do with her spoken request, is the key both to her thoughts and to His. If we do not understand His reply, we *may* misunderstand the miracle—certainly we are in danger of grievously misunderstanding Him—a far worse evil.

How many children are troubled in heart that Jesus should have spoken to His mother as our translation compels them to suppose He did speak! "O Woman, what have you to do with me? My hour has not yet come." His hour for working the miracle *had* come, for He wrought it; and if He had to do with one human soul at all, that soul must be His mother. The "woman," too, sounds strange in our ears. This last, however, is our fault: we allow words to sink from their high rank, and then put them to degraded uses. What word so full of grace and tender imagings to any true man as that one word! The Savior did use it to His mother; and when He called her *woman,* the good custom of the country and the time was glorified in the word as it came from His lips *fulfilled* of humanity; for those lips were the open gates of a heart full of infinite meanings. Hence whatever word He used had more of the human in it than that word had ever held before.

What He did say was this—"Woman, what is there common to you and me? My hour is not yet come." What! was not their humanity common to them? Had she not been fit, therefore chosen, to bear Him? Was she not His mother? But His words had no reference to the relation between them; they only referred to the present condition of her mind, or rather the nature of the thought and expectation which now occupied it. Her hope and His intent were at variance. There was no harmony between His thought and hers; and it was to that thought and that hope of hers that His words were now addressed. To paraphrase the words — and if I do so with reverence and for the sake of the spirit which is higher than the word, I think I am allowed to do so — "Woman, what is there in your thoughts now that is in sympathy with mine? Also, the hour that you are expecting is not come yet."

What, then, was in our Lord's thoughts? and what was in His mother's thoughts to call forth His words? She was thinking the time had come for making a show of His power — for revealing what a great man He was — for beginning to let that glory shine, which was, in her notion, to culminate in the grandeur of a righteous monarch — a second Solomon, who should set down the mighty in the dust, and exalt them of low degree. Here was the opportunity for working like a prophet of old, and revealing of what a mighty son she was the favored mother.

And of what did the glow of her face, the light in her eyes, and the tone with which she uttered the words, "They have no wine," make Jesus think? Perhaps of the decease which He must accomplish at Jerusalem. Perhaps of a throne of glory betwixt the two thieves. Certainly of a kingdom of heaven not such as filled her imagination, even although her heaven-descended Son was the king thereof.

A kingdom of exulting obedience, not of acquiescence, still less of compulsion, lay germed in His bosom, and He must be laid in the grave ere that germ could send up its first green lobes into the air of the human world. No throne, therefore, of earthly grandeur for Him! No triumph for His blessed mother such as she dreamed! There was nothing common in their visioned ends. Hence came the change of mood to Jesus, and hence the words that sound at first so strange, seeming to have so little to do with the words of His mother.

But no change of mood could change a feeling towards mother or friends. The former, although she could ill understand what He meant, never fancied in His words any unkindness to her. She, too, had the face of the speaker to read; and from that face came such answer to her prayer for her friends, that she awaited no confirming words, but in the confidence of a mother who knew her child, said at once to the servants. "Do whatever He tells you."

If any one object that I have here imagined too much, I would remark, first, that the records in the Gospel are very brief and condensed; second, that the germs of a true intelligence must lie in this small seed, and our hearts are the soil in which it must unfold itself; third, that we are bound to understand the story, and that the foregoing are the suppositions on which I am able to understand it in a manner worthy of what I have learned concerning Him. I am bound to refuse every interpretation that seems to me unworthy of Him, for to accept such would be to sin against the Holy Ghost. If I am wrong in my idea either of that which I receive or of that which I reject, as soon as the fact is revealed to me I must cast the one away and do justice to the other. Meantime this interpretation seems to me to account for our Lord's words in a manner He will not be displeased with even if it fail to reach the mark of the fact.

That St. John saw, and might expect such interpretation to be found in the story, barely as he has told it, will be rendered the more probable if we remember his own similar condition and experience when he and his brother James prayed the Lord for the highest rank in His kingdom, and received an answer which evidently flowed from the same feeling to which I have attributed that given on this occasion to His mother.

" 'Fill the jars with water.' And they filled them up to the brim. 'Now draw some out, and take it to the steward of the feast.' So they took it. 'You have kept the good wine until now.' " It is such a thing of course that, when our Lord gave them wine, it would be of the best, that it seems almost absurd to remark upon it. What the Father would make and will make, and that towards which He is ever working, is *the Best;* and when our Lord turns the water into wine it must be very good.

It is like His Father, too, not to withhold good wine because men abuse it. Enforced virtue is unworthy of the name. That men may rise above temptation, it is needful that they should have temptation. It is the will of Him who makes the grapes and the wine. Men will even call Jesus himself a wine-bibber. What matters it, so long as He works as the Father works, and lives as the Father wills?

I dare not here be misunderstood. God chooses that men should be tried, but let a man beware of tempting his neighbor. God knows how and how much, and where and when: man is his brother's keeper, and must keep him according to his knowledge. A man may work the will of God for others, and be condemned therein because he sought his own will and not God's. That our Lord gave this company wine, does not prove that He would have given any company wine. To some He refused even the bread they requested at His hands. Because He gave wine to the wedding-guests, shall man dig a pit at the corner of every street, that the poor may fall therein, spending their money for that which is not bread, and their labor for that which satisfies not? Let the poor man be tempted as God wills, for the end of God is victory; let not man tempt him, for his end is his neighbor's fall. Or at best he heeds not his neighbor's end for the sake of gain, and he shall receive according to his works.

The Significance of this Miracle

To him who can thank God with free heart for His good wine, there is a glad significance in the fact that our Lord's first miracle was this turning of water into wine. It is a true symbol of what He has done for the world in glorifying all things. With His divine alchemy He turns not only water into wine, but common things into radiant mysteries, yes, every meal into a eucharist, and the jaws of the sepulchre into an outgoing gate. I do not mean that He makes any change in the things or ways of God, but a mighty change in the hearts and eyes of men, so that God's facts and God's meanings become their faiths and their hopes.

The destroying spirit, who works in the commonplace, is ever covering the deep and clouding the high. For those who listen to that spirit great things cannot be. Such are there, but they cannot see them, for in themselves they do not aspire. They believe, perhaps, in the truth and grace of their first child: when they have spoiled him, they laugh at the praises of childhood. From all that is thus low and wretched, incapable and fearful, He who made the water into wine delivers men. He reveals heaven around them, God in all things, truth in every instinct, and evil withering and hope springing even in the path of the destroyer.

That the wine should be His first miracle, and that the feeding of the multitudes should be the only other creative miracle, will also suggest many thoughts in connection with the symbol He has left us of His relation to His brethren. In the wine and the bread of the eucharist, He reminds us how utterly He has given, is giving, Himself for the gladness and the strength of His Father's children. Yea more; for in that He is the radiation of the Father's glory, this bread and wine is the symbol of how utterly the Father gives Himself to His children, how earnestly He would have them partakers of His own being. If Jesus was the son of the Father, is it hard to believe that He should give men bread and wine?

It was not His power, however, but His glory, that Jesus showed forth in the miracle. His power could not be hidden, but it was a poor thing beside His glory. Yes, power in itself is a poor thing. If it could stand alone, which it cannot, it would be a horror. No amount of lonely power could create. It is the love that is at the root of power, the power of power, which alone can create. What then was this His glory? What was it that made Him glorious?

It was that, like His Father, He ministered to the wants of men. Had they not needed the wine, He would not have made it, even for the sake of whatever show of His power. The concurrence of man's need and His love made it possible for that glory to shine forth. It is for this glory most that we worship Him. But power is no object of adoration, and they who try to worship it are as slaves. Their worship is no real worship. Those who trembled at the thunder from the mountain went and worshipped a golden calf, but Moses went into the thick darkness to find his God.

How far the expectation of the mother Mary—that her son would, by majesty of might, appeal to the wedding guests, and arouse their enthusiasm for Himself—was from our Lord's thoughts may be well seen in the fact that the miracle was not beheld even by the ruler of the feast. So quietly was it done, so entirely without pre-intimation of His intent, so stolenly, as it were, in the two simple-ordered acts—the filling of the water-pots with water, and the drawing of it out again—as to make it manifest that it was done for the ministration. He did not do it even for the show of His goodness, but *to be good*. This alone could show His Father's goodness. It was done because here was an opportunity in which all circumstances combined with the bodily presence of the powerful and the prayer of His mother, to render it fit that the love of His heart should go forth in giving His merry-making brothers and sisters more and better wine to drink.

And herein we find another point in which this miracle of Jesus resembles the working of His Father. For God ministers to us so gently, so stolenly, as it were, with such a quiet, tender, loving absence of display, that men often drink of His wine, as these wedding guests drank, without knowing whence it comes—without thinking that the giver is beside them, yea, in their very hearts. For God will not compel the adoration of men: that would be but a pagan worship. He will rouse in men a sense of need, which shall grow at length into a longing; He will make them feel after Him, until by their search becoming able to hold Him, He may at length reveal to them the glory of their Father. He works silently—keeps quiet behind His works, as it were, that He may truly reveal Himself in the right time. With this intent also, when men find His wine good and yet do not rise and search for the giver, He will plague them with sore plagues, that the good wine of life may not be to them, and therefore to Him and the universe, an evil thing.

It would seem that the correlative of creation is search; that as God has *made* us, we must *find* Him. Thus our action must reflect His. Thus He glorifies us with a share in the end of all things, which is that the Father and His children may be one in thought, judgment, feeling, and intent, in a word, that they may mean the same thing. St. John says that Jesus thus "manifested His glory, and His disciples believed in Him." I doubt if any but His disciples knew of the miracle; or of those others who might see or hear of it. It is possible to see a miracle, and not believe in it; while many of those who saw a miracle of our Lord believed in the miracle, and yet did not believe in Him.

I wonder how many Christians there are who so thoroughly believe God made them that they can laugh in God's name; who understand that God invented laughter and gave it to His children. Such belief would add a keenness to the zest in their enjoyment, and slay that feeble laughter in which neither heart nor intellect has a share.

It would help them also to understand the depth of this miracle. The Lord of gladness delights in the laughter of a merry heart. These wedding guests could have done without wine, surely without more wine and better wine. But the Father looks with no esteem upon a bare existence, and is ever working, even by suffering, to render life more rich and plentiful. His gifts are to the overflowing of the cup;

but when the cup would overflow, He deepens its hollow, and widens its brim. Our Lord is profuse like His Father, yea, will, at His own sternest cost, be lavish to His brethren. He will give them wine indeed.

But even they who know whence the good wine comes, and joyously thank the giver, shall one day cry out, like the praiseful ruler of the feast to him who gave it not, "You have kept the good wine until now."

FOR THOUGHT & DISCUSSION

1. Why was Jesus present at the wedding in Cana? What does His very presence there reveal concerning Him?

2. What, apparently, were Mary's reasons for telling Jesus that the wine was gone? What were Jesus's reasons for responding to her as he did?

3. Why does MacDonald write, "I am bound to refuse every interpretation that seems to me unworthy of Him"? What are the dangers of a blind acceptance of the opinions of others, however widely held, concerning spiritual things?

4. What is meant by the statement: "Enforced virtue is unworthy of the name"? What is the relation between true virtue and free will?

5. In what sense is the spirit of "common things" a "destroying spirit," the enemy of true spirituality? How does this miracle help us to see "God in all things"?

6. Why is it horrible to think of God as pure power alone? What is the glory of God's power? Why is God so quiet and unobtrusive in expressing it?

7. What does it mean to be able to "laugh in God's name"? How is this not only consistent with, but an aid to, a proper understanding of God's purposes in our lives?

THREE

THE CURE
OF SIMON'S
WIFE'S MOTHER

(Matthew 8:14-15; Mark 1:29-31; Luke 4:38-39)

*I*n respect of the purpose I have in view, it is of little consequence in what order I take the miracles. I choose for my second chapter the story of the cure of St. Peter's mother-in-law. Bare as the narrative is, the event it records has elements which might have been moulded with artistic effect — on the one side the woman tossing in the folds of the fever, on the other the entering Life. But it is not from this side that I care to view it.

Neither do I wish to look at it from the point of view of the bystanders, although it would appear that we had the testimony of three of them in the three Gospels which contain the story. We might almost determine the position in the group about the bed occupied by each of the three, from the differences between their testimonies. One says

Jesus stood over her; another, He touched her hand; the third, He lifted her up: they agree that the fever left her, and she ministered to them. In the present case, as in others behind, I mean to regard the miracle from the point of view of the person healed.

Pain, sickness, delirium, madness, are as great infringements of the laws of nature as the miracles themselves. They are such veritable presences to the human experience, that what bears no relation to their existence cannot be the God of the human race. And the man who cannot find his God in the fog of suffering, no less than he who forgets his God in the sunshine of health, has learned little either of St. Paul or St. John.

So long as men must toss in weary fancies all the dark night, crying, "Would God it were morning," to find, it may be, when it arrives, but little comfort in the grey dawn, so long must we regard God as one to be seen or believed in — cried unto at least — across all the dreary flats of distress or dark mountains of pain. Therefore, those who would help their fellows must sometimes look for Him, as it were, through the eyes of those who suffer, and try to help them to think, not from ours, but from their own point of vision. I shall therefore now write almost entirely for those to whom suffering is familiar, or at least well known. And first I would remind them that all suffering is against the ideal order of things.

No man can love pain. It is an unlovely, an ugly, abhorrent thing. The more true and delicate the bodily and mental constitution, the more must it recoil from pain. No one, I think, could dislike pain so much as the Savior must have disliked it. God dislikes it. He is then on our side in the matter. He knows it is grievous to be borne, a thing He would cast out of His blessed universe, save for reasons.

But one will say, "How can this help me when the agony racks me, and the weariness rests on me like a gravestone?" Is it nothing, I answer, to be reminded that suffering is in its nature transitory, that it is against the first and final will of God, that it is a means only, not an end? Is it nothing to be told that it will pass away? Is not that what you would? God made man for lordly skies, great sunshine, gay colors, free winds, and delicate odors. However the fogs may be needful for the soul, right gladly does He send them away, and cause the dayspring from on high to revisit His children. While they suffer He is brooding over them an eternal day, suffering with them, but rejoicing in their future. He is the God of the individual man, or He could be no God of the race.

I believe it is possible—and that some have achieved it —so to believe in and rest upon the immutable Health that one regards his own sickness as a kind of passing aberration. The soul is thereby sustained, even as sometimes in a weary dream the man is comforted by telling himself it is but a dream, and that waking is sure. God would have us reasonable and strong. Every effort of His children to rise above the invasion of evil in body or in mind is a pleasure to Him. Few, I suppose, attain to this. But there is a better thing which to many, I trust, is easier — to say, "Thy will be done."

The Miracle

But now let us look at the miracle as received by the woman. She had "a great fever." She was tossing from side to side in vain attempts to ease a nameless misery. Her head ached, and forms dreary, even in their terror, kept rising before her in miserable and aimless dreams. Senseless words went on repeating themselves till her very brain was sick of them. She was destitute, afflicted, tormented. Through it all was the nameless unrest, not an aching, nor a burning, nor a stinging, but a bodily grief, dark, drear, and nameless. How could they have borne such before He had come?

A sudden ceasing of motions uncontrolled; a coolness gliding through the burning skin; a sense of waking into repose; a consciousness of all-pervading well-being, of strength conquering weakness, of light displacing dark-ness, of urging life at the heart; and behold! she is sitting up in her bed, a hand clasping hers, a face looking in hers. He has judged the evil thing, and it is gone. He has saved her out of her distresses. They fold away from off her like the cerements of death. She is new-born, new-made — all things are new-born with her — and He who makes all things new is there.

From Him, she knows, has the healing flowed. He has given of His life to her. Away, afar behind her floats the cloud of her suffering. She almost forgets it in her grateful joy. She is herself now. She rises. The sun is shining. It had been shining all the time — waiting for her. The lake of Galilee is glittering joyously. That too sets forth the law of life. But the fulfilling of the law is love: she rises and mini-sters.

I am tempted to remark in passing, although I shall have better opportunity of dealing with the matter involved, that there is no sign of those whom our Lord cures desiring to retain the privileges of the invalid. The joy of health is labor. He who is restored must be fellow-worker with God. This woman, lifted out of the whelming sand of the fever and set upon her feet, hastens to her ministrations. She has been used to hard work. It is all right now; she must do it again.

But who was He who had thus lifted her up? She saw a young man by her side. Is it the young man, Jesus, of whom she has heard? For Capernaum is not far from Nazareth, and the report of His wisdom and goodness must have spread, for He had grown in favor with man as well as with God. Is it He, to whom God has given such power, or is it John, of whom she has also heard? Whether He was a prophet or a son of the prophets, whether He was Jesus or John, she waits not to question; for here are guests; here is something to be done. Questions will keep; work must be dispatched. It is the day, and the night is at hand. She rose and ministered unto them.

God the Father Is Always Healing

But if we ask who He is, this is the answer: He is the Son of God come to do the works of His Father. Where, then, is the healing of the Father? All the world over, in every man's life and knowledge, almost in every man's personal experience, although it may be unrecognized as such. For just as in certain moods of selfishness our hearts are insensible to the tenderest love of our surrounding families, so the degrading spirit of the commonplace *enables* us to live in the midst of ministrations, so far from knowing them as such, that it is hard for us to believe that the very heart of God would care to do that which His hand alone can do and is doing every moment.

I remind my reader that I have taken it for granted that he confesses there is a God, or at least hopes there may be a God. If any one interposes, saying that science nowadays will not permit him to believe in such a being, I answer it is not for him I am now writing, but for such as have gone through a different course of thought and experience from his. To him I may be honored to say a word some day. I do not think of him now.

But to the reader of my choice I do say that I see no middle course between believing that every alleviation of pain, every dawning of hope across the troubled atmosphere of the spirit, every case of growing well again, is the doing of God, or that there is no God at all—none at least in whom *I* could believe. Had Christians been believing in God better, more grandly, the present phase of unbelief—which no doubt is needful, and must appear some time in the world's history—would not have appeared in our day. No doubt it has come when it must, and will vanish when it must; but those who do believe are more to blame for it, I think, than those who do not believe.

The common kind of belief in God is rationally untenable. Half to an insensate nature, half to a living God, is a worship that cannot stand. God is all in all, or no God at all.

The man who goes to church every Sunday, and yet trembles before chance is a Christian only because Christ has claimed him. He is not a Christian as having believed in Him. I would not be hard. There are so many degrees in faith! A man may be on the right track, may be learning of Christ, and be very poor and weak. But I say there is no *standing* room, no reality of reason, between absolute faith and absolute unbelief. Either not a sparrow falls to the ground without Him, or there is no God, and we are fatherless children. Those who attempt to live in such a limbo as lies between the two, are only driven of the wind and tossed.

Has my reader ever known the weariness of suffering, the clouding of the inner sky, the haunting of spectral shapes, the misery of disordered laws, when nature is wrong within him, and her music is out of tune and harsh, when he is shot through with varied griefs and pains, and it seems as there were no life more in the world, save of misery — "pain, pain ever, for ever"? Then, surely, he has also known the turn of the tide, when the pain begins to abate, when the sweet sleep falls upon soul and body, when a faint hope doubtfully glimmers across the gloom! This is His will, His law of life conquering the law of death.

Tell me not of natural laws, as if I were ignorant of them, or meant to deny them. The question is whether these laws go wheeling on of themselves in a symmetry of mathematical shapes, or whether their perfect order, their unbroken certainty of movement, is not the expression of a perfect intellect informed by a perfect heart. Law is truth: has it a soul of thought, or has it not? If not, then farewell hope and love and possible perfection. But for me, I will hope on, strive on, fight with the invading unbelief. For the horror of being the sport of insensate law — the more perfect the more terrible — is hell and utter perdition. If a man tells me that science says God is not a likely being, I answer, Probably not — such as you, who have given your keen, admirable, enviable powers to the observation of outer things only, are capable of supposing Him. But that the God I mean may not be the very heart of the lovely order you see so much better than I, you have given me no reason to fear. My God may be above and beyond and in all that.

In this matter of healing, then, as in all the miracles, we find Jesus doing the works of the Father. God is our Savior. The Son of God comes healing the sick — doing that, I repeat, before our eyes, which the Father, for His own reasons — some of which I think I can see well enough — does from behind the veil of His creation and its laws. The cure comes by law, comes by the physician who brings the law to bear upon us. We awake, and lo! it is God the Savior. Every recovery is as much His work as the birth of a child; as much the work of the Father as if it had been wrought by the word of the Son before the eyes of the multitude.

A God Indeed

Need I, to combat again the vulgar notion that the essence of miracles lies in their power, dwell upon this miracle further? Surely, no one who honors the Savior will for a moment imagine Him, as He entered the chamber where the woman lay tormented, saying to Himself, "Here is an opportunity of showing how mighty my Father is!" No. There was suffering; here was healing. What I could imagine Him saying to Himself would be, "Here I can help! Here my Father will let me put forth my healing, and give her back to her people."

What should we think of a rich man, who, suddenly brought into contact with the starving upon his own estate, should think within himself, "Here is a chance for me! Now I can let them see how rich I am!" and so plunge his hands in his pockets and lay gold upon the bare table? The receivers might well be grateful; but the arm of the poor neighbor put under the head of the dying man, would gather a deeper gratitude, a return of tenderer love.

It is heart alone that can satisfy heart. It is the love of God alone that can gather to itself the love of His children. To believe in an almighty being is hardly to believe in a God at all. To believe in a being who, in His weakness and poverty, if such could be, would die for His creatures, would be to believe in a God indeed.

For Thought and Discussion

1. What are the proper attitudes for the Christian to take towards suffering, when it comes?

2. What does it mean to want to "retain the privileges of an invalid" after one is healed? Why does this seem to be a serious temptation for some? How may they be helped?

3. In what sense may Christians be blamed for "the present phase of unbelief" in the world? What is meant by a Christian's needing to believe in God "better, more grandly"?

4. Interpret the statement: "To believe in an almighty being is hardly to believe in a God at all."

FOUR

MIRACLES OF HEALING UNSOLICITED

*I*n my last chapter I took the healing of Simon's wife's mother as a type of all such miracles, viewed from the consciousness of the person healed. In the multitude of cases—for it must not be forgotten that there was a multitude of which we have no individual record—the experience must have been very similar. The evil thing, the antagonist of their life, departed; they knew in themselves that they were healed. They beheld before them the face and form from whom the healing power had gone forth, and they believed in the man.

What they believed *about* Him, farther than that He had healed them and was good, I cannot pretend to say. Some said He was one thing, some another, but they believed in the man Himself. They felt henceforth the strongest of ties binding His life to their life. He was now the central thought of their being. Their minds lay open to all His influences, operating in time and by holy gradations. The well of life was henceforth to them an unsealed fountain, and endless currents of essential life began to flow from it through their existence. High love urging gratitude awoke the conscience to intenser life; and the healed began to recoil from evil deeds and vile thoughts as jarring with the new friendship. Mere acquaintance with a good man is a powerful antidote to evil; but the knowledge of *such* a man, as those healed by Him knew Him, was the mightiest of divine influences.

In these miracles of healing our Lord must have laid one of the largest of the foundation-stones of His church. The healed knew Him henceforth, not by comprehension, but with their whole being. Their very life acknowledged Him. They returned to their homes to recall and love afresh. I wonder what their talk about Him was like. What an insight it would give into our common nature, to know how these men and women thought and spoke concerning Him.

But the time soon arrived when they had to be public martyrs—that is, witnesses to what they knew, come of it what might. After our Lord's departure came the necessity for those who loved Him to gather together, thus bearing their testimony at once. Next to His immediate disciples, those whom He had cured must have been the very heart of the young church. Imagine the living strength of such a heart—personal love to the personal helper the very core of it. The church had begun with the first gush of affection in the heart of the mother Mary, and now "great was the company of those that published" the good news to the world.

The works of the Father had drawn the hearts of the children, and they spoke of the Elder Brother who had brought those works to their doors. The thoughtful remembrances of those who had heard Him speak; the grateful convictions of those whom He had healed; the tender memories of those whom He had taken in His arms and blessed — these were the fine fibrous multitudinous roots which were to the church existence, growth, and continuance. Individual life is the life of the church.

But one may say: Why then did He not cure all the sick in Judaea? Simply because all were not ready to be cured. Many would not have believed in Him if He had cured them. Their illness had not yet wrought its work, had not yet ripened them to the possibility of faith. His cure would have left them deeper in evil than before. "He did not do many mighty works there because of their unbelief." God will cure a man, will give him a fresh start of health and hope, and the man will be the better for it, even without having *yet* learned to thank Him. But to behold the healer and acknowledge the outstretched hand of help, yet not to believe in the healer, is a terrible thing for the man.

I think the Lord kept His personal healing for such as it would bring at once into some relation of heart and will with Himself. Thus arose His frequent demand of faith — a demand apparently always responded to. At the word, the flickering of belief, the smoking flax, burst into a flame. Evil, that is, physical evil, is a moral good — a mighty means to a lofty end. Pain is an evil; but a good as well, which it would be a great injury to take from the man before it had wrought its end. Then it becomes all evil, and must pass.

I now proceed to a group of individual cases in which, as far as we can judge from the narratives, our Lord gave the gift of restoration unsolicited. There are other instances of the same, but they fall into other groups, gathered because of other features.

The Woman with a Spirit of Infirmity (Luke 13:10-17)
The first is that, recorded by St. Luke alone, of the "woman who had a spirit of infirmity for eighteen years; she was bent over and could not fully straighten herself." It may be

that this belongs to the class of demoniacal possession as well, but I prefer to take it here; for I am very doubtful whether the expression in the narrative, "a spirit of infirmity," even coupled with that of our Lord in defending her and Himself from the hypocritical attack of the ruler of the synagogue, "this woman . . . whom Satan bound," renders it necessary to regard it as one of the latter kind. This is, however, a matter of small importance — at least from our present point of view.

Bowed earthwards, this woman had been in bondage eighteen years. Necessary as it is to one's faith to believe every trouble fitted for the being who has to bear it, every physical evil not merely the result of moral evil, but antidotal thereto, no one ought to dare judge of the relation between moral condition and physical suffering in individual cases. Our Lord has warned us from that. But in proportion as love and truth prevail in the hearts of men, physical evil will vanish from the earth. The righteousness of His descendants will destroy the disease which the unrighteousness of their ancestor has transmitted to them. But, I repeat, to destroy this physical evil save by the destruction of its cause, by the redemption of the human nature from moral evil, would be to ruin the world.

What in this woman it was that made it right she should bear these bonds for eighteen years, who can tell? Certainly it was not that God had forgotten her. What it may have preserved her from, one may perhaps conjecture, but can hardly have a right to utter. Neither can we tell how she had borne the sad affliction; whether in the lovely patience common amongst the daughters of affliction, or with the natural repining of one made to behold the sun, and doomed ever to regard the ground upon which she trod. While patience would have its glorious reward in the cure, it is possible that even the repinings of prideful pain might be destroyed by the grand deliverance, that gratitude might beget sorrow for vanished impatience. Anyhow, the right hour had come when the darkness must fly away.

Supported, I presume, by a staff, she had crept to the synagogue. There is no appearance from the story that she had come there to seek Jesus, or even that when in His presence she saw Him before the word of her deliverance had gone forth. Most likely, being bowed together, she heard Him before she saw Him.

But He saw her. Going to her, I think, and saying, "Woman, you are freed from your infirmity," "He laid His hands upon her, and immediately she was made straight, and she praised God." What an uplifting!—a type of all that God works in His human beings. The head, downbent with sin, care, sorrow, pain, is uplifted. We lift our eyes to God. We bend no longer even to His will, but raise ourselves up towards His will, for His will has become our will, and that will is our sanctification.

Although the woman did not beg the Son to cure her, she may have prayed the Father much. Anyhow, proof that she was ready for the miracle is not wanting. She glorified God. It is enough. She not merely thanked the man who had wrought the cure, for of this we cannot doubt; but she glorified the known Savior, God, from whom comes down every good gift and every perfect gift.

She had her share in the miracle I think too, as, in His perfect bounty, God gives a share to every one in what work He does for him. I mean that, with the given power, *she* had to *lift herself* up. Such active faith is the needful response in order that a man may be a child of God, and not the mere instrument upon which His power plays a soulless tune.

In this preventing of prayer, in this answering before the call, in this bringing of the blessing to the door, according to which I have grouped this with the following miracles, Jesus did as His Father is doing every day. He was doing the works of His Father. If men had no help, no deliverance from the ills which come upon them—even those which they bring upon themselves—except such as they prayed for, where would the world be? But the help of God is ever coming, ever setting them free whom Satan has bound, every giving them a fresh occasion and a fresh impulse to glorify the God of their salvation.

For with every such recovery the child in the man is new-born — for some precious moments at least. A gentleness of spirit, a wonder at the world, a sense of the blessedness of being, an openness to calm yet rousing influences, appear in the man. These are the descending angels of God. The passion that had blotted out the child will revive; the strife of the world will renew wrath and hate; ambition and greed will blot out the beauty of the earth; envy of others will blind the man to his own blessedness; and self-conceit will revive in him all those prejudices whose very strength lies in his weakness; but the man has had a glimpse of the peace, to gain which he must fight with himself. He has for one moment felt what he might be if he trusted in God, and the memory of it may return in the hour of temptation.

As the commonest things in nature are the most lovely, so the commonest agencies in humanity are the most powerful. Sickness and recovery therefrom have a larger share in the divine order of things for the deliverance of men than can show itself to the keenest eyes. Isolated in individuals, the facts are unknown; or, slow and obscure in their operation, are forgotten by the time their effects appear. Many things combine to render an enlarged view of the moral influences of sickness and recovery impossible. The kingdom comes not with observation, and the working of the leaven of its approach must be chiefly unseen. Like the creative energy itself, it works "in secret shadow, far from all men's sight."

The teaching of our Lord which immediately follows concerning the small beginnings of His kingdom, symbolized in the grain of mustard seed and the leaven, may, I think, have immediate reference to the cure of this woman, and show that He regarded her glorifying of God for her recovery as one of those beginnings of mighty growth. We do find the same similes in a different connection in St. Matthew and St. Mark. But even if we had no instances of fact, it would be rational to suppose that the Lord, in the varieties of place, audience, and occasion, in the dullness likewise of His disciples, and the perfection of the similes He chose, would again and again make use of the same.

The Man with the Withered Hand (Matt. 12:9-14; Mark 3:1-6; Luke 6:6-11)

I now come to the second miracle of the group, namely that, recorded by all the Evangelists except St. John, of the cure of the man with the withered hand. This, like the preceding, was done in the synagogue. And I may remark, in passing, that all of this group, with the exception of the last —one of very peculiar circumstance—were performed upon the Sabbath, and each gave rise to discussion concerning the lawfulness of the deed.

St. Mark says they watched Jesus to see whether He would heal the man on the Sabbath day. St. Luke adds that He knew their thoughts, and therefore met them with the question of its lawfulness. St. Matthew says they challenged Him to the deed by asking Him whether it was lawful. The mere watching could hardly have taken place without the man's perceiving something in motion which had to do with Him. But there is no indication of a request.

There cannot surely be many who have reached half the average life of man without at some time having felt the body a burden in some way, and regarded a possible deliverance from it as an enfranchisement. If the spirit of man were fulfilled of the Spirit of God, the body would simply be a living house, an obedient servant—yes, a humble mediator, by the senses, between his thoughts and God's thoughts. But when every breath has, as it were, to be sent for and brought hither with much labor and small consolation, when the withered limb hangs irresponsive, lost and cumbersome, then even the physical man understands his share in the groaning of the creation after the sonship.

When, at a word issuing from such a mouth as that of Jesus of Nazareth, the withered, distorted hand obeyed and became filled with its old human might, little would the man care that other men—even rulers of synagogues, even Scribes and Pharisees—should question the rectitude of Him who had healed him. The power which restored the gift of God and completed humanity, must be of God.

Argument upon argument might follow from old books and old customs and learned interpretations, wherein man set forth the will of God as different from the laws of His world, but the man whose hand was restored whole as the other, knew it fitting that his hands should match. They might talk; he would thank God for the crooked made straight. Bewilder his judgment they might with their glosses upon commandment and observance, but they could not keep his heart from gladness; and, being glad, whom should he praise but God? The hand was now as God had meant it to be. Nor could he behold the face of Jesus, and doubt that such a man would do only that which was right. It was not Satan, but God that had set him free.

Here, plainly by the record, our Lord gave the man his share, not of mere acquiescence, but of active will, in the miracle. If man is the child of God, he must have a share in the works of the Father. Without such share in the work as faith gives, cure will be of little avail. "Stretch out your hand," said the Healer; and the man made the effort. The withered hand obeyed, and was no more withered. *In* the act came the cure, without which the act had been confined to the will, and had never taken form in the outstretching. It is the same in all spiritual redemption.

Think for a moment with what delight the man would employ his new hand. This right hand would henceforth be God's hand. But was not the other hand God's too? — God's as much as this? Had not the power of God been always present in that left hand, whose unwithered life had ministered to him all these years? Was it not the life of God that inspired his whole frame? By the loss and restoration in one part, he would understand possession in the whole.

But as the withered and restored limb to the man, so is the maimed and healed man to his brethren. In every man the power by which he does the commonest things is the power of God. The power is not *of* us. Our power does it; but we do not make the power. This, plain as it is, remains, however, the hardest lesson for a man to learn with conviction and thanksgiving. For God has, as it were, put us just so far away from Him that we can exercise the divine thing in us, our own will, in returning towards our source. Then we shall learn the fact that we are infinitely more great and blessed in being the outcome of a perfect self-constituting will, than we could be by the conversion of any imagined independence of origin into fact for us. This is a truth no man *can* understand, feel, or truly acknowledge, save in proportion as he has become one with his perfect origin, the will of God.

While opposition exists between the thing made and the maker, there can be but discord and confusion in the judgment of the creature. No true felicitous vision of the facts of the relation between his God and him can exist. No perception of a unity such as cannot exist between independent wills, but only in unspeakable love and tenderness between the causing Will and the caused will, can yet have place. Those who cannot see how the human will should be free in dependence upon the will of God, have not realized that the will of God made the will of man. When most it pants for freedom, the will of man is the child of the will of God, and therefore there can be no natural opposition or strife between them. Nay, more, the whole labor of God is that the will of man should be free as His will is free — in the same way that His will is free — by the perfect love of the man for that which is true, harmonious, lawful, creative.

If a man say, "But might not the will of God make my will with the intent of over-riding and enslaving it?" I answer, such a Will could not create, could not be God, for it involves the false and contradictory. That would be to make a will in order that it might be no will. To create in order to uncreate is something else than divine. But a free will is not the liberty to do whatever one likes, but the power of doing whatever one sees ought to be done, even in the very face of otherwise overwhelming impulse. There lies freedom indeed.

The Man by the Pool of Bethzatha (John 5:2-18)

I come now to the case of the man who had been paralyzed for eight-and-thirty years. There is great pathos in the story. For many, at least, of these years, the man had haunted the borders of legendary magic, for I regard the statement about the angel troubling the pool as only the expression of a current superstition. Oh, how different from the healing of our Lord! What He had to bestow was free to all. The cure of no man by His hand weakened that hand for the cure of the rest. None were poorer that one was made rich.

But this legend of the troubling of the pool fostered the evil passion of emulation, and that in a most selfish kind. Nowhere in the divine arrangements is my gain another's loss. If it be said that this was the mode in which God determined which was to be healed, I answer that the effort necessary was contrary to all we admire most in humanity. Does the doctrine of Christ, and by that I insist we must interpret the ways of God, countenance a man's hurrying to be before the rest, and gain the boon in virtue of having the least need of it, inasmuch as he was the ablest to run and plunge first into the eddies left by the fantastic angel?

But the Master comes near. In Him the power of life rests as in "its own calm home, its crystal shrine," and he that believeth in Him shall not need to make haste. He knew it was time this man should be healed, and did not wait to be asked. Indeed the man did not know Him; did not even know His name. "Do you want to be healed?" "Sir, I have no man to put me into the pool and while I am going another steps down before me." "Rise, take up your pallet, and walk."

Our Lord delays the cure in this case with no further speech. The man knows nothing about Him, and He makes no demand upon his faith, except that of obedience. He gives him something to do at once. He will not find him again by and by. The man obeys, takes up his bed, and walks.

He sets an open path before us; *we* must walk in it. More, we must be willing to believe that the path is open, that we have strength to walk in it. God's gift glides into man's choice. It is needful that we should follow with our effort in the track of His foregoing power. To refuse is to destroy the gift. His cure is not for such as choose to be invalids. They must be willing to be made whole, even if it should involve the carrying of their beds and walking. Some keep in bed who have strength enough to get up and walk. There is a self-care and a self-pity, a laziness and conceit of incapacity, which are as unhealing for the body as they are unhealthy in the mind, corrupting all dignity and destroying all sympathy.

Some invalids are not cured because they will not be healed. They will not stretch out the hand; they will not rise; they will not walk; above all things, they will not work. Labor is not in itself an evil like the sickness, but often a divine, a blissful remedy. Nor is the duty or the advantage confined to those who ought to labor for their own support. No amount of wealth sets one free from the obligation to work — in a world the God of which is ever working. He who does not know what to do has never seriously asked himself what he ought to do.

But there is a class of persons, the very opposite of these, who, as extremes meet, fall into a similar fault. They will not be healed either. They will not take the repose God gives to His beloved. Some sicknesses are to be cured with rest, others with labor. The right way is all—to meet the sickness as God would have it met, to submit or to resist according to the conditions of cure. Whatsoever is not of faith is sin; and she who will not go to her couch and rest in the Lord, is to blame even as she who will not rise and go to her work.

There is reason to suppose that this man had brought his infirmity upon himself—I do not mean by the mere neglect of physical laws, but by the doing of what he knew to be wrong. For the Lord, although He allowed the gladness of the deliverance full sway at first, when He found him afterwards did not leave him without the lesson that all health and well-being depend upon purity of life: "See, you are well! Sin no more, that nothing worse befall you." It is the only case of recorded cure in which Jesus gives a warning of the kind. Therefore I think the probability is as I have stated it. Hence, the fact that we may be ourselves to blame for our sufferings is no reason why we should not go to God to deliver us from them. David the king knew this, and set it forth in that grand poem, the 107th Psalm.

The Man Blind from Birth (John 9:1-41)

In the very next case we find that Jesus will not admit the cause of the man's condition, blindness from his birth, to be the sin either of the man himself, or of his parents. The probability seems, to judge from their behavior in the persecution that followed, that both the man and his parents were people of character, thought, and honorable prudence. He was born blind, Jesus said, "that the works of God might be made manifest in him." What works, then?

The work of creation for one, rather than the work of healing. The man had suffered nothing in being born blind. God had made him only not so blessed as his fellows, with the intent of giving him equal faculty and even greater enjoyment afterwards, with the honor of being employed for the revelation of His works to men. In him Jesus created sight before men's eyes. For, as at the first God said, "Let there be light," so the work of God is still to give light to the world, and Jesus must work His work, and *be* the light of the world.

Jesus saw the man, the disciples asked their question, and He had no sooner answered it, than "he spat on the ground and made clay of the spittle and anointed the man's eyes with the clay." Why this mediating clay? Why the spittle and the touch? Because the man who could not see Him must yet be brought into sensible contact with Him. He must know that the healing came from the man who touched him. Our Lord took pains about it because the man was blind. And for the man's share in the miracle, having blinded him a second time as it were with clay, He sends him to the pool to wash it away: clay and blindness should depart together by the act of the man's faith. It was as if the Lord said, "I blinded you: now, go and see."

But who can imagine, save in a conception only less dim than the man's blindness, the glory which burst upon him when, as the restoring clay left his eyes, the light of the world invaded his astonished soul? The very idea may well make one tremble: Blackness of darkness! . . . . The glory of celestial blue! The towers of the great Jerusalem dwelling in the awful space! The room! The life! The tenfold-glorified being! Any wonder might follow on such a wonder.

But the best remained behind. A man had said, "I am the light of the world," and lo! here was the light of the world. The words had been vague as a dark form in darkness, but now the thing itself had invaded his innermost soul. But the face of the man who was this light of the world he had not seen. It is no wonder then when Jesus found him and asked him, "Do you believe in the Son of man?" he should reply,

"Who is he, sir, that I may believe in him?" He was ready. He had only to know which was He, that he might worship Him. Here at length was the Light of the world before him — the man who had said, "I am the light of the world," and straightway the world burst upon him in light! Would this man ever need further proof that there was indeed a God of men? I suspect he had a grander idea of the Son of God than any of his disciples as yet.

In this miracle as in all the rest, Jesus did in little the great work of the Father; for how many more are they to whom God has given the marvel of vision than those blind whom the Lord enlightened! What a divine *invention,* what a mighty gift of God is this very common thing — these eyes to see with — that light which enlightens the world, this sight which is the result of both. What a believer the man born blind must have become! Nothing should be too grand and good for him to believe thereafter — not even the doctrine hardest to commonplace humanity, though the most natural and reasonable to those who have beheld it — that the God of the light is a faithful, loving, upright, honest, and self-denying being, utterly devoted to the uttermost good of those whom He has made.

Such is the Father of lights who enlightens the world and every man that comes into it. Every pulsation of light on every brain is from Him. Every feeling of law and order is from Him. Every hint of right, every desire after the true, whatever we call aspiration, all longing for the light, every perception that this is true, that that ought to be done, is from the Father of lights. His infinite and varied light gathered into one point — for how can we speak at all of these things if we do not speak in figures? — concentrated and embodied in Jesus, became *the* light of the world. For the light is no longer only diffused, but in Him man "beholds the light *and whence it flows.*"

Not merely is our chamber enlightened, but we see the lamp. And so we turn again to God, the Father of lights, yea even of The Light of the World. Henceforth we know that all the light wherever diffused has its center in God, as the light that enlightened the blind man flowed from its center in Jesus. In other words, we have a glimmering, faint, human perception of the absolute glory. We know what God is in recognizing Him as our God.

Jesus did the works of the Father.

The Man with the Dropsy (Luke 15:1-6)

The next miracle — recorded by St. Luke alone — is the cure of the man with the dropsy, wrought also upon the Sabbath, but in the house of one of the chief of the Pharisees. There our Lord had gone to an entertainment, apparently large, for the following parable is spoken "to those who were invited, when He marked how they chose the places of honor." Hence the possibility at least is suggested, that the man was one of the guests. No doubt their houses were more accessible than ours, and it also was not difficult for one uninvited to make his way in, especially upon occasion of such a gathering.

But I think the word translated *before him* means *opposite to him* at the table; and that the man was not too ill to appear as a guest. The "took him and healed him and let him go," of our translation, is capable of meaning that He sent him away; but such is not the meaning of the original. That merely implies that He *took him,* went to him and laid His hands upon him, thus connecting the cure with Himself, and then released him, set him free, took His hands off him, turning at once to the other guests and justifying Himself by appealing to their own righteous conduct towards the ass and the ox. I think the man remained reclining at the table, to enjoy the appetite of health at a good meal.

The Slave's Ear Restored (Luke 22:47-53)

I come now to the last of the group, exceptional in its nature, inasmuch as it was not the curing of a disease or natural defect, but the reparation of an injury, or hurt at least, inflicted by one of his own followers. This miracle also is recorded by St. Luke alone. The other evangelists relate the occasion of the miracle, but not the miracle itself; They record the blow, but not the touch. I shall not, therefore, compare their accounts, which have considerable variety, but no inconsistency. I shall confine myself to the story as told by St. Luke.

Peter, intending, doubtless, to cleave the head of a servant of the high priest who had come out to take Jesus, with unaccustomed hand, probably trembling with rage and perhaps with fear, missed his well-meant aim, and only cut off the man's ear. Jesus said, "No more of this!" with the words, "He touched his ear and healed him." Hardly had the wound reached the true sting of its pain, before the gentle hand of Him whom the servant had come to drag to the torture, dismissed the agony as if it had never been.

Whether He restored the ear, or left the loss of it for a reminder to the man of the part he had taken against his Lord, and the return the Lord had made him, we do not know. Neither do we know whether he turned back ashamed and contrite, now that in his own person he had felt the life that dwelt in Jesus, or followed out the capture to the end. Possibly the blow of Peter was the form which the favor of God took, preparing the way, like the blindness from the birth, for the glory that was to be manifested in him. But our Lord would countenance no violence done in His defense. They might do Him as they would. If His Father would not defend Him, neither would He defend Himself.

Within sight of the fearful death that awaited Him, His heart was no less hardened to the pain of another. Neither did it make any difference that it was the pain of an enemy —even an enemy who was taking Him to the cross. There was suffering; here was healing. He came to do the works of Him that sent Him. He did good to them that hated Him, for His Father is the Savior of men, saving "them out of their distresses."

For Thought and Discussion

Why did not the Lord heal all the sick in Judaea? Under what conditions would healing a person possibly harm him? Explain.

The Woman with a Spirit of Infirmity:

1. Why is it essential that we always refrain from judging as to the "relation between moral condition and physical suffering in individual cases"? What is the proper Christian attitude in this regard?

2. What are the effects upon the human spirit when it recognizes the unsolicited, unprayed for works of God?

The Man with the Withered Hand:

1. Explain the statement: "If man is the child of God, he must share in the works of the Father."

2. What is "the hardest lesson for a man to learn with conviction and thanksgiving"? Put in your own words what MacDonald is saying here about the freedom of our wills in relation to the power and purposes of God in creating us.

The Man by the Pool of Bethzatha:

1. How may self-care and self-pity oppose the blessings God would otherwise give? How may these attitudes be recognized and dismissed?

2. What is the proper Christian attitude toward work? rest? self-blame?

The Man Blind from Birth:

What are the "works of God" that are made manifest in this incident?

The Man with the Dropsy:

Why do you think Christ performed so many of these unsolicited miracles on the Sabbath Day?

The Slave's Ear Restored:

What admonitions for our own conduct towards those who oppose us may we take from this incident?

FIVE

MIRACLES OF HEALING SOLICITED BY THE SUFFERERS

I come now to the second group of miracles, those granted to the prayers of the sufferers. But before I make any general remarks on the specialty of these, I must speak of one case which appears to lie between the preceding group and this. It involves peculiar difficulties, in connection with the facts which render its classification uncertain.

The Woman with a Flow of Blood (Luke 8:40-48)
At Capernaum, apparently, our Lord was upon His way with Jairus to visit his daughter, accompanied by a crowd of people who had heard the request of the ruler of the synagogue. A woman who had been ill for twelve years came behind Him and touched the hem of His garment.

This we may regard as a prayer in so far as she came to Him, saying within herself, "If I only touch His garment, I shall be made well." But, on the other hand, it was no true prayer in as far as she expected to be healed without the knowledge and will of the healer. Although she came to Him, she did not ask Him to heal her. She thought with innocent theft to steal from Him a cure.

What follows according to St. Matthew's account, occasions me no difficulty. He does not say that the woman was cured by the touch; he says nothing of her cure until Jesus had turned and seen her, and spoken the word to her, whereupon he adds: "And instantly the woman was made well." But St. Mark and St. Luke represent that the woman was cured upon the touch, and that the cure was only confirmed afterwards by the words of our Lord. They likewise represent Jesus as ignorant of what had taken place, except in so far as He knew that, without His volition, some cure had been wrought by contact with His person, of which He was aware by the passing from Him of a saving influence. By this, in the heart of a crowd which pressed upon Him so that many must have come into bodily contact with Him, He knew that some one had touched Him with special intent.

The difficulty is that the woman could be cured by the garment of Jesus, without (not against) the will of Jesus. I think that the whole difficulty arises from our ignorance — a helpless ignorance — of the relations of thought and matter. I use the word *thought* rather than spirit, because in reflecting upon spirit (which is thought), people generally represent to themselves a vague form of matter. All religion is founded on the belief or instinct — call it what we will — that matter is the result of mind, spirit, thought. The relation between them is therefore simply too close, too near for us to understand. Here is what I am able to suggest concerning the account of the miracle as given by St. Mark and St. Luke.

Who can tell what cure may lie in a perfect body, informed, yea, caused, by a perfect spirit? If stones and plants can heal by the will of God in them, might there not dwell in the perfect health of a body, in which dwelt the Son of God, a necessarily healing power? It may seem that in the fact of the many crowding about Him, concerning whom we have no testimony of influence received, there lies a refutation of this supposition. But who can tell what He may have done even for them without their recognizing it save in conscious well-being? Besides, those who crowded nearest Him would mostly be of the strongest who were least in need of a physician.

And who can tell how the faith of the heart, calming or arousing the whole nature, may have rendered the very person of the woman more fit than the persons of others in the crowd to receive the sacred influence? For although she did not pray, she had the faith as alive though as small as the mustard seed. Why might not health from the fountain of health flow then into the empty channel of the woman's weakness? It may have been so.

In the preceding remarks I have anticipated a chapter to follow—a chapter of speculation, which may God make humble and right. But some remark was needful here. What must be to some a far greater difficulty has yet to be considered. It is the representation of the Lord's ignorance of the cure, save from the reaction upon His own person of the influence which went out from Him.

Omniscience is a consequence, not an essential of the divine nature. God knows because He creates. The Father knows because He orders. The Son knows because He obeys. The knowledge of the Father must be perfect; such knowledge the Son neither needs nor desires. His sole care is to do the will of the Father. Herein lies His essential divinity. Although He knew that one of His apostles should betray Him, I doubt much whether, when He chose Judas, He knew that he was that one. We must take His own words as true. Not only does He not claim perfect knowledge, but He disclaims it. He speaks once, at least, to His Father with an *if it be possible.* Those who believe omniscience essential to divinity, will therefore be driven to say that Christ was not divine. This will be their punishment for placing knowledge on a level with love. No one who does so can worship in spirit and in truth, can lift up his heart in pure adoration. He will suppose he does, but his heaven will be in the clouds, not in the sky.

But now we come to the holy of holies of the story — the divinest of its divinity. Jesus could not leave the woman with the half of a gift. He could not let her go away so poor. She had stolen the half: she must fetch the other half — come and take it from His hand. That is, she must know who had healed her. Her will and His must come together; and for this her eyes and His, her voice and His ears, her ears and His voice must meet. It is the only case recorded in which He says *Daughter.* It could not have been because she was younger than Himself; there could not have been much difference between their ages in that direction. Let us see what lies in the word.

With the modesty belonging to her as a woman, intensified by the painful shrinking which had its origin in the peculiar nature of her suffering, she dared not present herself to the eyes of the Lord, but thought merely to gather from under His table a crumb unseen. And I do not believe that our Lord in calling her had any desire to make her tell her tale of grief, and, in her eyes, of shame. It would have been enough to Him if she had come and stood before Him, and said nothing. Nor had she to appear before His face with only that poor remnant of strength which had sufficed to bring her to the hem of His garment behind Him; for now she knew in herself that she was healed of her plague, and the consciousness must have been strength.

Yet she trembled when she came. Filled with awe and gratitude, she could not stand before Him; she fell down at

His feet. There, hiding her face in her hands, I presume, she forgot the surrounding multitude, and was alone in the chamber of her consciousness with the Son of Man. Her love, her gratitude, her holy awe unite in an impulse to tell Him all.

When the lower approaches the higher in love, even between men, the longing is to be known; the prayer is "Know me." This was David's prayer to God, "Search me and know me." There should be no more concealment. Besides, painful as it was to her to speak, He had a right to know all, and know it He should. It was her sacrifice offered unto the Lord. She told Him all the truth. To conceal anything from Him now would be greater pain than to tell all, for the thing concealed would be as a barrier between Him and her. And He accepted the offering. He let her speak, and tell all.

But it was painful. He understood it well. His heart yearned towards the woman to shield her from her own innocent shame. Her story appealed to all that was tenderest in humanity; for the secret which her modesty had hidden, her conscience had spoken aloud. Therefore the tenderest word that the language could afford must be hers. "Daughter," He said. It was the fullest reward, the richest acknowledgement He could find of the honor in which He held her, His satisfaction with her conduct, and the perfect love He bore her.

The degrading spirit of which I have spoken, the spirit of the commonplace, which lowers everything to the level of its own capacity of belief, will say that the word was an eastern mode in more common use than with us. I say that whatever Jesus did or said, He did and said like other men, and He did and said as no other man did or said. If He said *Daughter,* it meant what any man would mean by it; it also meant what no man could mean by it—what no man was good enough, great enough, loving enough to mean by it. In Him the Father spoke to this one the eternal truth of His relation to all His daughters, to all the women He has made, though individually it can be heard only by those who lift up the filial eyes, lay bare the filial heart.

I think also that very possibly come compunction arose in her mind, the moment she knew herself healed, at the mode in which she had gained her cure. Hence when the Lord called her she may have thought He was offended with her because of it. Possibly her contrition for the little fault, if fault indeed it was, may have increased the agony of feeling with which she forced rather than poured out her confession. But he soothes her with gentle, consoling, restoring words: "Take heart. Go in peace, and be healed of your disease." Nay, more, He attributes her cure to her own faith. "Your faith has made you well." What wealth of tenderness! She must not be left in her ignorance to the danger of associating power with the mere garment of the divine. She must be brought face to face with her healer. Her faith was an ignorant faith, but, however obscured in her consciousness, it was a true faith. She believed in the man, and our Lord loved the modesty that kept her from pressing into His presence. It may indeed have been the very strength of her faith working in her ignorance that caused her to extend His power even to the skirts of His garments. And there He met the ignorance, not with rebuke, but with the more grace. When did He ever quench the smoking flax? See how He praises her. He is never slow to commend. The first quiver of the upturning eyelid is to Him faith. He commands the feeblest faith in the ignorant soul, rebukes it as little only in apostolic souls where it ought to be greater. "Your faith has saved you." However poor it was, it was enough for that. Between death and the least movement of life there is a gulf wider than that fixed between the gates of heaven and the depths of hell. He said *"Daughter."*

The Cleansing of the Leper (Matthew 8:1-4; Mark 1:40-45; Luke 5:12-16)

I come now to the first instance of plain request, that of the leper who fell down before Him saying, "Lord, if you will you can make me clean"—a prayer lovely in the simplicity of its human pleading. His power was the man's claim. The relation between them was of the strongest—that between plenty and need, between strength and weakness, between health and disease. In regard to God, all whose power is creative, any necessity of His creature is a perfect bond between them and Him. His magnificence must flow into the channels of the indigence He has created.

Observe how Jesus responds in the terms of the man's request. The woman found the healing where she sought it —in the hem of His garment. One man says, "Come with me"; the Lord goes. Another says, "I am not worthy to have you come under my roof", the Lord remains. Here the man says, "If you will"; the Lord answers, "I will." But He goes far beyond the man's request.

I need say nothing of the grievous complaint under which he labored. It made of the man an outcast and ashamed. No one would come near him lest he should share his condemnation. Physical evil had, as it were, come to the surface in him. He was "full of leprosy." Men shrink more from skin-diseases than from any other.*

Jesus could have cured him with a word. There was no need He should touch him. No *need* did I say? There was every need. For no one else would touch him. The healthy human hand, always more or less healing, was never laid on him; he was despised and rejected. It was a poor thing for the Lord to cure his body; He must comfort and cure his sore heart. Out went the loving hand to the ugly skin, and there was His brother as he should be—with the flesh of a child. I thank God that the touch went before the word.

---

*And they are amongst the hardest to cure; just as the skin-diseases of the soul linger long after the heart is greatly cured. Witness the petulance, fastidiousness, censoriousness, social self-assertion, general disagreeableness of so many good people—all in the moral skin—repulsive exceedingly. I say *good* people; I do not say *very good*, nor do I say Christ-*like*, for that they are not. (MacDonald himself suffered from eczema—Ed.)

That touch was more than the healing. It was to the leper what the word *Daughter* was to the woman in the crowd, what the *Neither do I* was to the woman in the temple — the sign of the perfect presence. Outer and inner are one with Him: the outermost sign is the revelation of the innermost heart.

The Lord gave him something to do at once, and something not to do. He was to go to the priest, and to hold his tongue. It is easier to do than to abstain. He went to the priest; he did not hold his tongue.

That the Lord should send him to the priest requires no explanation. The sacred customs of his country our Lord in His own person constantly recognized. That He saw in them more than the priests themselves was no reason for passing them by. The testimony which He wished the man to bear concerning Him lay in the offering of the gift which Moses had commanded. His healing was in harmony with all the forms of the ancient law; for it came from the same source, and would in the lapse of ages complete what the law had but begun. This the man was to manifest for Him.

The only other thing He required of him — silence — the man would not, at least did not, yield. The probability is that he needed the injunction for his own sake more than for the Master's sake; that he was a talkative, demonstrative man, whose better life was ever in danger of evaporating in words. The Lord required silence of him, that he might think, and give the seed time to root itself well before it shot its leaves out into the world.

Are there not some in our own day, who, having had a glimpse of truth across the darkness of a moral leprosy, instantly begin to blaze abroad the matter, as if it were their part at once to call to their fellows, and teach them out of an intellectual twilight — in which they can as yet see men only as trees walking — instead of retiring into the wilderness, for a time at least, to commune with their own hearts, and be still? But he meant well, nor is it any wonder that such a man should be incapable of such a sacrifice. The Lord had touched him. His nature was all in commotion with gratitude. His self-conceit swelled high. His tongue would not be still. Perhaps he judged himself a leper favored above his fellow-lepers. Nothing would more tend to talkativeness than such a selfish mistake. He would be grateful. He would befriend his healer against His will.

He would work for Him—alas! only to impede the labors of the Wise; for the Lord found His popularity a great obstacle to the only success He sought. "He went out and began to talk freely about it, and to spread the news, so that Jesus could no longer openly enter a town." His nature could not yet understand the kingdom that comes not with observation, and from presumption mingled with affection, he would serve the Lord after a better fashion than that of doing His will. And he had his reward. He had his share in bringing his healer to the cross.

Obedience is the only service.

The Cleaning of Ten Lepers (Luke 17:11-19)
I take now the cure of the ten lepers, done apparently in a village of Galilee towards Samaria. They stood at a distance in a group, probably afraid of offending Him by any nearer approach, and cried aloud, "Jesus, Master, have mercy on us." Instead of at once uttering their cure, He desired them to go and show themselves to the priests, partly perhaps for the justification of His own mission, but more certainly for the sake of the men themselves, that He might, in accordance with His frequent practice, give them something wherein to be obedient.

It served also, as the sequel shows, to individualize their relation to Him. The relation as a group was not sufficient for the men. Between Him and them it must be the relation of man to man. Individual faith must, as it were, break up the group—to favor a far deeper reunion. Its bond was now a common suffering; it must be changed to a common faith in the healer of it.

His intention wrought in them at first but small apparent result. They obeyed, and went to go to the priests, probably wondering whether they would be healed or not, for the beginnings of faith are so small that they can hardly be recognized as such. Going, they found themselves cured. Nine of them held on their way, obedient; while the tenth, forgetting for the moment in his gratitude the word of the Master, turned back and fell at His feet. A moral martinet, a scribe, or a Pharisee, might have said "The nine were right, the tenth was wrong: he ought to have kept to the letter of the command." Not so the Master: he accepted the gratitude as the germ of an infinite obedience.

Real love is obedience and all things beside. The Lord's own devotion was that which burns up the letter with the consuming fire of love, fulfilling and setting it aside. High love needs no letter to guide it. Doubtless the letter is all that weak faith is capable of, and it is well for those who keep it! But it is ill for those who do not outgrow and forget it! Forget it, I say, *by outgrowing it.* The Lord cared little for the letter of His own commands; He cared all for the spirit, for that was life.

This man was a stranger, as the Jews called him, a Samaritan. Therefore the Lord praised him to his followers. It was as if he had said, "See, Jews, who think yourselves the great praisers of God! Here are ten lepers cleansed: where are the nine? One comes back to glorify God—a Samaritan!" To the man himself He says, "Rise and go your way; your faith has made you well." Again this commending of individual faith! "Was it not the faith of the others too that had healed them?" Doubtless. If they had had enough to bring them back, He would have told them that their faith had saved them. But they were content to be healed, and until their love, which is the deeper faith, brought them to the Master's feet, their faith was not ripe for praise.

But it was not for their blame, it was for the Samaritan's

praise that He spoke. Probably this man's faith had caused the cry of all the ten. Probably he was the salt of the little group of outcasts—the tenth, the righteous man. Hence they were contented, for the time, with their cure: he forgot the cure itself in his gratitude. A moment more, and with obedient feet he would overtake them on their way to the priest.

I may not find a better place for remarking on the variety of our Lord's treatment of those whom He cured; that is, the variety of the form in which He conveyed the cure. In the record I do not think we find two cases treated in the same manner. There is no massing of the people with Him. In His behavior to men, just as in their relation to His Father, every man is alone with Him. In this case of the ten, as I have said, I think He sent them away, partly, that this individuality might have an opportunity of asserting itself. They had stood afar off; therefore, He could not lay the hand of love on each. But now one left the group and brought his gratitude to the Master's feet, and with a loud voice glorified God the Healer.

In reflecting then on the details of the various cures we must seek the causes of their diversity mainly in the differences of the persons cured, not forgetting, at the same time, that all the accounts are brief, and that our capacity is poor for the task. The whole divine treatment of man is that of a father to his children—only a father infinitely more a father than any man can be. Before Him stands each, as much an individual child as if there were no one but him. The relation is awful in its singleness. Even when God deals with a nation as a nation, it is only when by this dealing the individual is aroused to a sense of his own wrong, that he can understand how the nation has sinned, or can turn himself to work a change. The nation cannot change save as its members change; and the few who begin the change are the elect of that nation.

All that is precious in the individual heart depends for

existence on the relation the individual bears to other individuals: alone—how can he love? alone—where is his truth? It is for and by the individuals that the individual lives. A community is the true development of individual relations. Its very possibility lies in the conscience of its men and women. No setting right can be done in the *mass*. There are no masses save in corruption.

In a word, the man, in virtue of standing alone in God, stands *with* his fellows, and receives from them divine influences without which he cannot be made perfect. It is in virtue of the living consciences of its individuals that a common conscience is possible to a nation.

I cannot work this out here, but I would avoid being misunderstood. Although I say, every man stands alone in God, I yet say two or many can meet in God as they cannot meet save in God. Only in God can two or many truly meet; only as they recognize their oneness with God can they become one with each other.

In the variety then of His individual treatment of the sick, Jesus did the works of His Father *as* His Father does them. For the Spirit of God speaks to the spirit of the man, and the Providence of God arranges everything for the best good of the individual—counting the very hairs of his head. Every man had a cure of his own; every woman had a cure of her own—all one and the same in principle, each individual in the application of the principle. This was the foundation of the true church. And yet the members of that church will try to separate upon individual and unavoidable differences!

But once more the question recurs: Why say so often that this and that one's faith had saved him? Was it not enough that He had saved them?—Our Lord would knit the bond between Him and each man by arousing the man's individuality, which is, in deepest fact, his conscience. The cure of a man depended upon no uncertain or arbitrary movement of the feelings of Jesus. He was always ready to heal.

No one was ever refused who asked Him. It rested with the man: the healing could not have its way and enter in, save the man would open his door. It was there for him if he would take it, or rather when he would allow Him to bestow it. Hence the question and the praise of the patient's faith.

There was no danger then of that diseased self-consciousness which nowadays is always asking, "Have I faith? Have I faith?" searching, in fact, for grounds of self-confidence, and turning away the eyes in the search from the only source whence confidence can flow—the natal home of power and love. How shall faith be born but of the beholding of the faithful? This diseased self-contemplation was not indeed a Jewish complaint at all, nor possible in the bodily presence of the Master. Hence the praise given to a man's faith could not hurt him; it only made him glad and more faithful still. This disease itself is in more need of His curing hand than all the leprosies of Judaea and Samaria.

The Two Blind Men (Matthew 9:27-31)

The cases which remain of this group are of blind men—the first, that recorded by St. Matthew of the two who followed Jesus, crying, "Have mercy on us, Son of David." He asked them if they believed that He was able to do the thing for them, drawing, I say, the bond between them closer thereby. They said they did believe it, and at once He touched their eyes—again the bodily contact, as in the case of the blind man already considered—especially needful in the case of the blind, to associate the healing with the healer.

But there are differences between the cases. The man who had not asked to be healed was as it were put through a longer process of cure—I think that his faith and his will might be called into exercise; and the bodily contact was made closer to the development of his faith and will. He made clay and put it on his eyes, and the man had to go and wash. Where the prayer and the confession of faith reveal the spiritual contact already effected, the cure is immediate.

"According to your faith," the Lord said, "be it done to you."

On these men, as on the leper, He laid the charge of silence, by them, as by him, sadly disregarded. The fact that He went into the house, and allowed them to follow Him there before He cured them, also shows that He desired in their case, doubtless because of circumstances, to avoid publicity, a desire which they foiled. Their gladness overcame, if not their gratitude, yet the higher faith that is one with obedience. When the other leper turned back to speak his gratitude, it was but the delay of a moment in the fulfilling of the command. But the gratitude that disobeys an injunction, that does what the man is told not to do, and so plunges into the irretrievable, is a virtue that needs a development amounting almost to a metamorphosis.

Blind Bartimaeus (Matthew 20:29-34; Mark 10:46-52; Luke 18:35-43)

In the one remaining case there is a slight confusion in the records. St. Luke says that it was performed as Jesus entered into Jericho; St. Mark says it was as He went out of Jericho, and gives the name and parentage of the blind beggar. Indeed his account is considerably more minute than that of the others. St. Matthew agrees with St. Mark as to the occasion, but says there were two blind men. We shall follow the account of St. Mark.

Bartimaeus, having learned the cause of the tumultuous passing of feet, calls, like those former two blind men, upon the Son of David to have mercy on him.* The multitude finds fault with his crying and calling. I presume he was noisy in his eagerness after his vanished vision, and the multitude considered it indecorous. Or perhaps the rebuke

---

*In these two cases, the cry is upon the *Son of David:* I wonder if this had come to be considered by the blind the correct formula of address to the new prophet. But the cases are almost too few to justify even a passing conjecture at generalization.

arose from that common resentment of a crowd against any one who makes himself what they consider unreasonably conspicuous, claiming a share in the attention of the potentate to which they cannot themselves pretend.

But the Lord stops, and tells them to call the man; and some of them, either being his friends, or changing their tone when the great man takes notice of him, begin to congratulate and comfort him. He, casting away his garment in his eagerness, rises, and is led through the yielding crowd to the presence of the Lord. To enter in some degree into the personal knowledge of the man before curing him, and to consolidate his faith, Jesus, the tones of whose voice were full of the life of God (the cultivated hearing of a blind man would be best able to interpret), began to talk a little with him.

"What do you want me to do for you?"

"Master, let me receive my sight."

"Go your way; your faith has made you well."

Immediately he saw; and the first use he made of his sight was to follow Him who had given it.

Neither St. Mark nor St. Luke, whose accounts are almost exactly the same, says that He touched the man's eyes. St. Matthew says He touched the eyes of the *two* blind men whom his account places in otherwise identical circumstances. With a surrounding crowd who knew them, I think the touching was less necessary than in private; but there is no need to inquire which is the more correct account. The former two may have omitted a fact, or St. Matthew *may* have combined the story with that of the two blind men already noticed, of which he is the sole narrator. But in any case there are, I think, but two recorded instances of the blind praying for cure. Most likely there were more, perhaps there were many such.

Remarks on prayer

I have now to consider, as suggested by the idea of this

group, the question of prayer generally; for Jesus did the works of Him who sent Him: as Jesus did so God does.

I have not seen an argument against what is called the efficacy of prayer which appears to me to have any force but what is derived from some narrow conception of the divine nature. If there be a God at all, it is absurd to suppose that His ways of working should be such as to destroy His side of the highest relation that can exist between Him and those whom He has cared to make — to destroy, I mean, the relation of the will of the creator to the individual will of His creature.

That God should bind Himself in an iron net of His own laws — that His laws should bind Him in any way, seeing they are just His nature in action — is sufficiently absurd. But that He should, with an unchangeable order of material causes and effects, cage in for ever the winged aspirations of the human will which He has made in the image of His own will, towards its natural air of freedom in His will, would be pronounced inconceivable, were it not that it has been conceived and uttered — conceived and uttered, however, only by minds to which the fact of this relation was, if at all present, then only in the vaguest and most incomplete form.

It is far easier to believe that as both — the laws of nature, namely, and the human will — proceed from the same eternally harmonious thought, they too are so in harmony, that for the perfect operation of either no infringement upon the other is needful; and that what seems to be such infringement would show itself to a deeper knowledge of both as a perfectly harmonious co-operation.

Nor would it matter that we know so little, were it not that with each fresh discovery we are so ready to fancy anew that now, at last, we know all about it. We have neither humility enough to be faithful, nor faith enough to be humble. Unfit to grasp any whole, yet with an inborn idea of wholeness which ought to be our safety in urging us ever on towards the Unity, we are constantly calling each new part the whole, saying we have found the idea, and casting ourselves on the couch of self-glorification. Thus the very need of unity is by our pride perverted to our ruin. We say we have found it, when we have it not.

Hence, also, it becomes easy to refuse certain considerations, yea, certain facts, a place in our system—for the system will cease to be a system at all the moment they are acknowledged. They may have in them the very germ of life and truth; but what is that, if they destroy this Babylon that we have built? Are not its forms stately and fair? Yea, *can* there be statelier and fairer?

The main point is simply this, that what it would not be well for God to give before a man had asked for it, it may be not only well, but best, to give when he has asked.* I believe that the first half of our training is up to the asking point; after that the treatment has a grand new element in it. For God can give when a man is in the fit condition to receive it, what He cannot give before because the man cannot receive it.

How give instruction in the harmony of colors and tones to a man who cannot yet distinguish between shade and shade or tone and tone, upon which distinction all harmony depends? A man cannot receive except another will give. No more can a man give if another will not receive; he can only offer. Doubtless, God works on every man, else he *could* have no divine tendency at all. There would be no *thither* for him to turn his face towards; there could be at best but a sense of want. But the moment the man has given in to God—the spirit for which he prays can work in him completely *with* him, not now (as it *appeared* then) *against* him.

Every parent at all worthy of the relation must know that occasions occur in which the asking of the child makes the giving of the parent the natural correlative. In a

Well and *Best* must be the same things with God when He acts.

way infinitely higher, yet the same at the root—for all is of
God—He can give when the man asks what He could not
give without. In the latter case the man would take only the
husk of the gift, and cast the kernel away—a husk poison-
ous without the kernel, although wholesome and comforting with it.

But some will say, "We may ask, but it is certain we shall
not have everything we ask for."

No, thank God, certainly not; we shall have nothing
which we ourselves, when capable of judging and choosing
with open eyes to its true relation to ourselves, would not
wish and choose to have. If God should give otherwise, it
must be as a healing punishment of inordinate and hurtful
desire.

The parable of the father dividing his living at the prayer
of the younger son, must be true of God's individual sons,
else it could not have been true of the Jews on the one hand
and the Gentiles on the other. He will grant some such
prayers because He knows that the swine and their husks
will send back His son with quite another prayer on his lips.
If my supposed interlocuter answers, "What then is the
good of praying, if it is not to go by what I want?" I can only
answer, "You have to learn, and it may be by a hard road."

In the kinds of things which men desire, there are essential differences. In physical well-being, there is a divine
good. In sufficient food and raiment, there is a divine fitness. In wealth, as such, there is *none*. A man may pray for
money to pay his debts, for healing of sickness which incap-
acitates him for labor or good work, for just judgment in the
eyes of his fellow-men, with an altogether different confidence from that with which he could pray for wealth, or for
bodily might to surpass his fellows, or for vengeance upon
those whose judgment of his merits differed from his own.
Although even then the divine soul will with his Savior say,
"If it be possible: Not my will but thine." For he will know
that God gives only the best.

"But God does not even cure every one who asks Him. And so with the other things you say are good to pray for."

Jesus did not cure all the ills in Judaea. But those He did cure were at least real ills and real needs. There was a fitness in the condition of some, a fitness favored by His own bodily presence amongst them, which met the virtue ready to go out from Him. But God is ever present, and I have yet to learn that any man prayed for money to be honest with and to meet the necessities of his family, and did the work of Him who had called him from the market-place of the nation, who did not receive his penny-a-day.

If to any one it seems otherwise, I believe the apparent contradiction will one day be cleared up to his satisfaction. God has not to satisfy the judgment of men as they are, but as they will be and must be, having learned the high and perfectly honest and grand way of things which is His will. For God to give men just what they want would often be the same as for a man to give gin to a night-wanderer whom he had it in his power to take home and set to work for wages.

But I must believe that many of the ills of which men complain would be speedily cured if they would work in the strength of prayer. If the man had not taken up his bed when Christ bade him, he would have been a great authority with the scribes and chief priests against the divine mission of Jesus. The power to work is a diviner gift than a great legacy. But these are individual affairs to be settled individually between God and His child. They cannot be pronounced upon generally because of individual differences. But here as there, now as then, the lack is *faith*.

A man may say, "How can I have faith?" I answer, "How can you indeed, who do the thing you know you ought not to do, and have not begun to do the thing you know you ought to do? How should you have faith? It is not well that you should be cured yet. It would have hurt these men to cure them if they would not ask. And you do not pray." The man who has prayed most is, I suspect, the least doubtful whether God hears prayer now as Jesus heard it then. That we doubt is well, for we are not yet in the empyrean of simple faith.

But I think the man who believes and prays now, has answers to his prayers even better than those which came to the sick in Judaea. For although the bodily presence of Jesus made a difference in their favor, I do believe that the Spirit of God, after widening its channels for nearly nineteen hundred years, can flow in greater plenty and richness now. Hence the answers to prayer must not only not be of quite the same character as then, but they must be better, coming yet closer to the heart of the need, whether known as such by him who prays, or not. But the change lies in man's power of reception, for God is always the same to His children. Only, being infinite, He must speak to them and act for them in the endless diversity which their growth and change render necessary. Thus only they can receive of His fulness who is all in all and unchangeable.

In our imperfect condition both of faith and of understanding, the whole question of asking and receiving must necessarily be surrounded with mist and the possibility of a mistake. It can be successfully encountered only by the man who for himself asks and hopes. It lies in too lofty regions and involves too many unknown conditions to be reduced to formulas of ours. God must do only the best, and man is greater and more needy than himself can know.

Yet he who asks *shall* receive — of the very best. One promise without reserve, and only one, because it includes all, remains: the promise of the Holy Spirit to them who ask it. He who has the Spirit of God, God Himself, in him, has the Life in him, possesses the final cure of all ill, has in himself the answer to all possible prayer.

For Thought and Discussion

The Woman with a Flow of Blood:

Explain the statement: "Her faith was an ignorant faith, but . . . it was a true faith." In what sense was it ignorant? true? Why did Christ call her "Daughter"?

The Cleansing of the Leper:

1. Explain the statement: "His magnificence must flow into the channels of the indigence He has created."

2. In the footnote, why does MacDonald refer to certain attitudes as "skin diseases of the soul"? Is this an apt metaphor? Why or why not?

3. Why does Christ require silence of the healed leper? Under what conditions is a more tacit testimony better than a more talkative one? Is this invariably true?

The Cleansing of the Ten Lepers:

1. What is meant by "outgrowing" the letter of a command? When may an abrogation of a command possibly be commendable? What cautions must be observed?

2. Why is God so careful to honor individual differences in His dealings with man? What are the implications of this principle for Christian community?

3. In what sense is the preoccupation "Have I faith?" a disease? What is the cure?

Two Blind Men:

How is the disregard of Christ's command here blameworthy, when the behavior of the tenth leper in Luke 17 was praised?

On Prayer:

1. What considerations should govern our asking things of God in prayer?

2. What encouragements for us to pray are contained in this section?

3. How is the promise of Luke 11:13 the crowning promise concerning prayer?

SIX

MIRACLES GRANTED TO THE PRAYER OF FRIENDS

*I*f we allow that prayer may in any case be heard for the man himself, it almost follows that it must be heard for others. It cannot well be in accordance with the spirit of Christianity, whose essential expression lies in the sacrifice of its founder, that a man should be heard only when he prays for himself. The fact that in cases of the preceding group faith was required on the part of the person healed as essential to his cure, represents no different principle from that which operates in the cases of the present group.

True, in these the condition is not faith on the part of the person cured, but faith on the part of him who asks for his cure. But the possession of faith by the patient was not in the least essential, as far as the power of Jesus was concerned, to his bodily cure, although no doubt favorable to it. It was necessary only to that spiritual healing, that higher cure, for the sake of which chiefly the Master brought about the lower.

In both cases, the requisition of faith is for the sake of those who ask — whether for themselves or for their friends, it matters not. It is a word to draw into closer contact with Himself. He cured many without such demand, as his Father is ever curing without prayer. Cure itself shall sometimes generate prayer and faith. Well, therefore, might the cure of others be sometimes granted to prayer.

Beyond this, however, there is a great fitness in the thing. For so are men bound together, that no good can come to one but all must share in it. The children suffer for the father, the father suffers for the children, and they are also blessed together. If a spiritual good descend upon the heart of a leader of the nation, the whole people might rejoice for themselves, for they must be partakers of the unspeakable gift.

To increase the faith of the father may be more for the faith of the child, healed in answer to his prayer, than anything done for the child himself. It is an enlarging of one of the many channels in which the divinest gifts flow. For those gifts chiefly, at first, flow to men through the hearts and souls of those of their fellows who are nearer the Father than they, until at length they are thus brought themselves to speak to God face to face.

A man may feel lonely in his highest moments of spiritual vision, when, in his simplest consciousness of duty, he turns his face towards the one Father, his own individual maker and necessity of his life. He may painfully feel that the best beloved understands not as he understands, feels not as he feels. Yet, he is, in his most isolated adoration of the Father of his spirit, nearer every one of the beloved than when eye meets eye, hand seeks by varied pressure to tell the emotion within.

The man who prays, in proportion to the purity of his prayer, becomes a spiritual power through whom power anew goes forth upon his fellows. He is a redistributor, as it were, of the divine blessing. Not in the exercise of his own will—that is the cesspool towards which all notions of priestly mediation naturally sink—but as the self-forgetting, God-loving brother of his kind, who would be in the world as Christ was in the world.

When a man prays for his fellow-man, for wife or child, mother or father, sister or brother or friend, the connection between the two is so close in God, that the blessing begged may well flow to the end of the prayer. Such a one then is, in his poor, far-off way, an advocate with the Father, like his master, Jesus Christ, The Righteous. He takes his friend into the presence with him, or if not into the presence, he leaves him with but the veil between them, and they touch through the veil.

The Official's Son (John 4:46-54)
The first instance we have in this kind, occurred at Cana, in the center of Galilee, where the first miracle was wrought. It is the second miracle in St. John's record, and is recorded by him only. Doubtless these two had especially attracted His nature—the turning of water into wine, and the restoration of a son to his father. The Fatherhood of God created the fatherhood in man; God's love man's love. And what shall he do to whom a son is given whom yet he cannot keep? The divine love in his heart cleaves to the child, and the child is vanishing! What can this nobleman do but seek the man of whom such wondrous rumors have reached his ears?

Between Cana and Tiberias, from which came the father with his prayer, was somewhere about twenty miles.

"He is at the point of death," said the father.

"Unless you see signs and wonders you will not believe," said Jesus.

"Sir, come down before my child dies."

"Go, your son will live."

If the nobleman might have understood the remark the Lord made, he was in no mood for principles, and respectfully he expostulates with our Lord for spending time in words when the need was so urgent. The sun of his life was going down into the darkness. He might deserve reproof, but even reproof has its season. "Sir, come down before my child dies." Whatever the Lord meant by the words, He urged it no farther. He sends him home with the assurance of the boy's recovery, showing him none of the signs or wonders of which He had spoken.

Had the man been of unbelieving kind he would have concluded, when he returned and found that all had occurred in the most natural fashion, that neither here had there been sign nor wonder, and would have gradually reverted to his old carelessness as to a higher will and its ordering of things below. But instead of this, when he heard that the boy began to get better the very hour when Jesus spoke the word—a fact quite easy to set down as a remarkable coincidence—he believed, and all his people with him. Probably he was in ideal reality the head of his house, the main source of household influences. If he was such, then he was a man of faith, for, where a man does not himself look up to the higher, the lower will hardly look faithfully up to him—surely a fit man to intercede for his son, with all his house ready to believe with him.

It may be said they too shared in the evidence—such as it was—not much of a sign or wonder to them. True, but people are not ready to believe the best evidence except they are predisposed in the direction of that evidence. If it be said, "they should have thought for themselves," I answer—To think with their head was no bad sign that they did think for themselves. A great deal of what is called freedom of thought is merely the self-assertion which would persuade itself of a freedom it would possess but cannot

without an effort too painful for ignorance and self-indul-
gence. The man would *feel* free without being free. To
assert one's individuality is not necessarily to be free: it *may*
indeed be but the outcome of absolute slavery.

But if this nobleman was a faithful man, whence our
Lord's word, "Unless you see signs and wonders you will not
believe"? I am not sure. It may have been as a rebuke to
those about him. This man — perhaps, as is said, a nobleman of Herod's court — may not have been a pure-bred
Jew, and hence our Lord's remark would bear an import
such as He uttered more plainly in the two cases following,
that of the Greek woman, and that of the Roman centurion:
"Unless *you* see signs and wonders you will not believe; *but
this man —.*"

With this meaning I should probably have been content,
were it not that the words were plainly addressed to the
man. I do not think this would destroy the interpretation,
for the Lord may have wished to draw the man out, and
make him, a Gentile or doubtful kind of Jew, rebuke the
disciples. Only the man's love for his son stood in the way.
He could think of nothing, speak of nothing save his son.
But it makes it unsatisfactory. And indeed I prefer the
following interpretation, because we have the other meaning in other places; also because this is of universal application, and to us of these days appears to me of special significance and value, applying to the men of science on the
one hand, and the men of superstition on the other.

My impression is, that our Lord, seeing the great faith of
the nobleman, grounded on what he had heard of the
Master from others, chiefly of His signs and wonders, did in
this remark require of him a higher faith still. It sounds to
me an expostulation with him. To express in the best way
my feeling concerning it, I would dare to imagine our Lord
speaking in this fashion:

"Why did you not pray the Father? Why do you want always to *see*? The door of prayer has been open since ever

God made man in His own image. Why are signs and wonders necessary to your faith? But I will do just as my Father
would have done if you had asked Him. Only when I do it, it
is a sign and a wonder that you may believe; and I wish you
could believe without it. But believe then for the very work's
sake, if you cannot believe for the word and the truth's sake.
Go your way, your son lives."

I would not be understood to say that the Lord *blamed*
him, or others in him, for needing signs and wonders: it was
rather, I think, that the Lord spoke out of the fulness of His
knowledge to awake in them some infant sense of what
constituted all His life — the presence of God. The order of
creation, the goings on of life, were ceaselessly flowing from
the very heart of the Father. Why should they seek signs
and wonders differing from common things only in being
uncommon? In essence there was no difference. Un-
commonness is not excellence, even as commonness is not
inferiority. The sign, the wonder is, in fact, the lower thing,
granted only because of men's hardness of heart and
slowness to believe — in itself of inferior nature to God's
chosen way.

Yet, if signs and wonders could help them, have them
they should, for neither were they at variance with the holy
laws of life and faithfulness. They were but less usual utter-
ances of the same. "Go your way: your son lives." The man,
nobleman certainly in this, obeyed, and found his obedience justify his faith.

But his son would have to work out his belief upon
grounds differing from those his father had. In himself he
could but recognize the resumption of the *natural* sway of
life. He would not necessarily know that it was God working
in him. For the cause of his cure, he would only hear the
story of it from his father — good evidence — but he himself
had not seen the face of the Holy One as his father had. In
one sense or another, he must seek and find Him. Every
generation must do its own seeking and its own finding.

The fault of the fathers often is that they expect their finding to stand in place of their children's seeking. They expect the children to receive that which has satisfied the need of their fathers upon their testimony; whereas rightly, their testimony is not ground for their children's belief, only for their children's search. That search is faith in the bud. No man can be sure till he has found it for himself. All that is required of the faithful nature is a willingness to seek.

In this case, as in the two which follow, the Lord heals from a distance. I have not much to remark upon this. There were reasons for it; one perhaps the necessity of an immediate answer to the prayer; another probably lay in its fitness to the faith of the supplicants. For to heal thus, although less of a sign or a wonder to the unbelieving, had in it an element of finer power upon the faith of such as came not for the sign or the wonder, but for the cure of the beloved. For he who loves can believe what he who loves not cannot believe; and he who loves most can believe most.

In this respect, these cures were like the healing granted to prayer in all ages—not that God is afar off, for He is closer to every man than his own conscious being is to his unconscious being—but that we receive the aid from the Unseen. Though there be no distance with God, it looks like it to men, and when Jesus cured thus, He cured with the same appearances which attended God's ordinary healing.

The Daughter of the Syrophoenician Woman (Matthew 15:21-28; Mark 7:24-30)

The next case I take up is similar. It belongs to another of my classes, but as a case of possession, there is little distinctive about it, while as the record of the devotion of a mother to her daughter—a devotion quickening in her faith so rare and lovely as to delight the very heart of Jesus with its humble intensity—it is one of the most beautiful of all the stories of healing.

The woman was a Greek, and had not had the traning of the

Jew for a belief in the Messiah. Her misconceptions concerning the healer of whom she had heard must have been full of fancies derived from the legends of her race. But she had yet been trained to believe, for her mighty love of her own child was the best power for the development of the child-like in herself.

She came crying to Him. About Him stood His disciples, proud of being Jews. For their sakes this chosen Gentile must be pained a little further, must bear with her Savior her part of suffering for the redemption even of His chosen apostles. They counted themselves the children, and such as she the dogs. He must show them the divine nature dwelling in her. For the sake of this revelation He must try her sorely, but not for long.

"Have mercy on me," she cried, "O Lord, Son of David; my daughter is severely possessed by a demon."

But not a word of reply came from the lips of the Healer. His disciples must speak first. They must supplicate for their Gentile sister. He would arouse in them the disapproval of their own exclusiveness, by putting it on for a moment that they might see it apart from themselves.

Their hearts were moved for the woman.

"Send her away," they said, meaning, "Give her what she wants." But to move the heart of love to grant the prayer, they—poor intercessors—added a selfish reason to justify the deed of goodness, either that they would avoid being supposed to acknowledge her claim on a level with that of a Jewess, and would make of it what both Puritans and priests would call "an uncovenanted mercy," or that they actually thought it would help to overcome the scruples of the Master. Possibly it was both. "She is crying after us," they said, meaning, "She is troublesome." They would have Him give as the ungenerous and the unjust give to the importunate.

But no healing could be granted on such a ground—not even to the prayer of an apostle. The woman herself must give a better.

"I was sent only," He said, "to the lost sheep of the house of Israel."

They understood the words falsely. We know that He did come for the Gentiles, and He was training them to see what they were so slow to understand, that He had other sheep which were not of this fold. He had need to begin with them thus early. Most of the troubles of His latest, perhaps greatest apostle, came from the indignation of Jewish Christians that he preached the good news to the Gentiles as if it had been originally meant for them. They would have had them enter into its privileges by the gates of Judaism.

What they did at length understand by these words is expressed in the additional word of our Lord given by St. Mark: "Let the children first be fed." But even this they could not understand until afterwards. They could not see that it was for the sake of the Gentiles as much as the Jews that Jesus came to the Jews first.

For whatever glorious exceptions there were amongst the Gentiles, surpassing even similar amongst Jews; and whatever the widespread refusal of the Jewish nation, He *could* not have been received amongst the Gentiles as amongst the Jews. In Judaea alone could the leaven work; there alone could the mustard-seed take fitting root. Once rooted and up, it would become a great tree, and the birds of the world would nestle in its branches. It was not that God loved the Jews more than the Gentiles that He chose them first, but that He must begin somewhere: *why*, God Himself knows, and perhaps has given us glimmerings.

Upheld by her God-given love, not yet would the woman turn away. Even such hard words as these could not repulse her.

She came now and fell at His feet. It is as the Master would have it. She presses only the nearer, she insists only the more; for the devil has a hold of her daughter.

"Lord, help me," is her cry; for the trouble of her daughter is her own. The "Help *me*" is far more profound and pathetic than the most vivid blazon of the daughter's sufferings.

But He answered and said,

"It is not right to take the children's bread and throw it to the dogs."

Terrible words! More dreadful far than any He ever spoke besides! Surely now she will depart in despair! But the Lord did not mean in them to speak *His* mind concerning the relation of Jew and Gentile. For not only do the future of His church and the teaching of His Spirit contradict it, but if He did mean what He said, then he acted as was unmeet, for He did cast a child's bread to a dog. No. He spoke as a Jew felt, that the elect Jews about Him might begin to understand that in Him is neither Jew nor Gentile, but all are brethren.

And He has gained His point. The spirit in the woman has been divinely goaded into utterance, and out come the glorious words of her love and faith, casting aside even insult itself as if it had never been — all for the sake of a daughter. Now, indeed, it is as He would have it.

"Yes, Lord, yet even the dogs eat the crumbs that fall from their master's table."

Or, as St. Matthew gives it:

"Yes Lord, yet even the dogs eat the crumbs that fall from their master's table."

A retort quite Greek in its readiness, its symmetry, and its point! But it was not the intellectual merit of the answer that pleased the Master. Cleverness is cheap. It is the faith He praises,* which was precious as rare — unspeakably precious even when it shall be the commonest thing in the universe, but precious now as the first fruits of a world

---

*Far more precious than any show of the intellect, even in regard of the intellect itself. The quickness of her answer was the scintillation of her intellect under the glow of her affection. Love is the quickening nurse of the whole nature. Faith in God will do more for the intellect at length than all the training of the schools. It will make the best that can be made of the whole man.

redeemed—precious now as coming from the lips of a Gentile—more precious as coming from the lips of a human mother pleading for her daughter.

"O woman, great is your faith: be it done for you as you desire."

Or, as St. Mark gives it, for we cannot afford to lose a varying word,

"For this saying you may go your way; the demon has left your daughter."

The loving mother has conquered the tormenting devil. She has called in the mighty aid of the original love. Through the channel of her love it flows, new-creating, "and her daughter was healed instantly."

Where, O disciples, are your children and your dogs now? Is not the wall of partition henceforth destroyed? No; you too have to be made whole of a worse devil, that of personal and national pride, before you understand. But the day of the Lord is coming for you, notwithstanding you are so incapable of knowing the signs and signals of its approach that, although its banners are spread across the flaming sky, it must come upon you as a thief in the night.

For the woman, we may well leave her to the embraces of her daughter. They are enough for her now. But endless more will follow, for God is exhaustless in giving where the human receiving holds out. God be praised that there are such embraces in the world! that there are mothers who are the salvation of their children!

The Centurion's Servant (Matthew 8:5-13; Luke 7:1-10)

We now complete a little family group, as it were, with the story of another foreigner, a Roman officer, who besought the Lord for his servant. This captain was at Capernaum at the time, where I presume he had heard of the cure which Jesus had granted to the nobleman for his son. It seems almost clear from the quality of his faith, however, that he must have heard much besides of Jesus—enough to give him matter of pondering for some time, for I do not think such humble confidence as his could be, like Jonah's gourd, the growth of a night.

He was evidently a man of noble and large nature. Instead of lording it over the subject Jews of Capernaum, he had built them a synagogue. His behavior to our Lord is marked by that respect which, shown to any human being, but especially to a person of lower social condition, is one of the surest marks of a finely wrought moral temperament. Such a nature may be beautifully developed by a military training, in which obedience and command go together. The excellence of faith and its instant response in action, would be more readily understood by the thoughtful officer of a well-disciplined army than by any one to whom organization was unknown.

Hence arose the parallel the centurion draws between his own and the Master's position, which so pleased the Lord by its direct simplicity. But humble as the man was, I doubt if anything less than some spiritual perception of the nobility of the character of Jesus, some perception of that which was altogether beyond even the power of healing, could have generated such perfect reverence, such child-like confidence as his. It is no wonder the Lord was pleased with it, for that kind of thing must be just what His Father loves.

According to St. Luke, the Roman captain considered himself so unworthy of notice from the carpenter's son — they of Capernaum, which was "his own city," knew his reputed parentage well enough — that he got the elders of the Jews to go and beg for him that He would come and heal his servant. They bore testimony to his worth, specifying that which would always be first in the eyes of such as they, that he loved their nation, and had built them a synagogue. Little they thought how the Lord was about to honor him above all their nation and all its synagogues. He went with them at once.

But before they reached the house, the centurion had had a fresh inroad of that divine disease, humility,* and had sent other friends to say,

"Lord, do not trouble yourself, for I am not worthy to have you come under my roof; therefore I did not presume to come to you. But say the word, and let my servant be healed. For I am a man set under authority, with soldiers under me: and I say to one, 'Go,' and he goes; and to another, 'Come,' and he comes; and to my slave, 'Do this,' and he does it."

This man was a philosopher. He ascended from that to which he was accustomed to that to which he was not accustomed. Nor did his divine logic fail him. He begins with acknowledging his own subjection, and states his own authority. Then he leaves it to our Lord to understand that he recognizes in Him an authority beyond all, expecting the powers of nature to obey their Master, just as his soldiers or his servants obey him. How grandly he must have believed in Him!

But beyond suspicion of flattery, he avoids the face of the man whom in heart he worships. How unlike those who press into the presence of a phantom-greatness! "A poor creature like me go and talk to Him!" the Roman captain would exclaim. "No, I will worship from afar off." And it is to be well heeded that the Lord went no further—turned at once. With the tax-gatherer Zacchaeus he would go home, if but to deliver him from the hopelessness of his self-contempt; but what occasion was there here? It was all right here. The centurion was one who needed but to go on.

In heart and soul he was nearer the Lord now than any of the disciples who followed Him. Surely some one among the elders of the Jews, his friends, would carry him the report of what the Master said. It would not hurt him. The praise of the truly great will do no harm, save it fall where it

---

*In him it was almost morbid, one might be tempted to say, were it not that it was sister to such mighty faith.

ought not, on the heart of the little. The praise of God never falls wrong, therefore never does any one harm. The Lord even implies we ought to seek it. His praise would but glorify the humility and the faith of this Roman by making both of them deeper and nobler still.

There is something very grand in the Lord's turning away from the house of the man who had greater faith than any He had found in Israel. Such were the words He spoke to those who followed Him, of whom in all likelihood the messenger elders were nearest. Having turned to say them, He turned not again but went His way. St. Luke, whose narrative is in other respects much fuller than St. Matthew's (who says that the centurion himself came to Jesus, and makes no mention of the elders), does not represent the Master as uttering a single word of cure, but implies that He just went away marvelling at him; while "when those who had been sent, returned to the house, they found the slave well." If any one ask how Jesus could marvel, I answer, Jesus could do more things than we can well understand. The fact that He marvelled at the great faith, shows that He is not surprised at the little, and therefore is able to make all needful and just, yea, and tender allowance.

Here I cannot do better for my readers than give them four lines, dear to me, but probably unknown to most of them, written, I must tell them, for the sake of their loving catholicity, by an English Jesuit of the seventeenth century. They touch the very heart of the relation between Jesus and the centurion: —

> *Thy God was making haste into thy roof;*
> *Thy humble faith and fear keeps Him aloof:*
> *He'll be thy guest; because He may not be,*
> *He'll come — into thy house? No, into thee.*

As I said, we thus complete a kind of family group, for surely the true servant is one of the family: we have the prayer of a father for a son, of a mother for a daughter, of a master for a servant. Alas! the dearness of this latter bond is not now known as once. There never was a rooted institution in parting with which something good was not lost for a time, however necessary its destruction might be for the welfare of the race. There are fewer free servants love their masters and mistresses now, I fear, than there were Roman bondsmen and bondswomen who loved theirs. And, on the other hand, very few masters and mistresses regard the bond between them and their servants with half the respect and tenderness with which many among the Romans regarded it. Slavery is a bad thing and of the devil, yet mutual jealousy and contempt are worse. But the time will yet come when a servant will serve for love as more than wages; and when the master of such a servant will honor him even to the making him sit down to meat, and coming forth and serving him.

The Paralytic (Matthew 9:1-8; Mark 2:1-12; Luke 5:17-26)
The next is the case of the palsied man, so graphically given both by St. Mark and St. Luke, and with less of circumstance by St. Matthew. This miracle also was done in Capernaum, called His own city. Pharisees and doctors of the law from every town in the country, hearing of His arrival, had gathered to Him, and were sitting listening to His teaching. There was no possibility of getting near Him, and the sick man's friends had carried him up to the roof, taken off the tiles, and let him down into the presence. It should not be their fault if the poor fellow was not cured.

"Jesus seeing their faith — When Jesus saw their faith — And when He saw their faith, He said to the paralytic, 'Take heart, my son' — 'Son' — 'Man, your sins are forgiven you.' " The forgiveness of the man's sins is by all of the narrators connected with the faith of his friends. This is very remarkable. The only other instance in which similar words are recorded, is that of the woman who came to Him in Simon's house, concerning whom He showed first, that her love was a sign that her sins were already forgiven.

They had brought the man to Him; to them He forgave his sins. He looked into his heart, and probably saw, as in the case of the man whom he cured by the pool of Bethesda, telling him to go and sin no more, that his own sins had brought upon him this suffering, a supposition which aids considerably to the understanding of the consequent conversation. He saw, at all events, that the assurance of forgiveness was what he most needed, whether because his conscience was oppressed with a sense of guilt, or that he must be brought to think more of the sin than of the suffering.

It involved an awful rebuke to the man, if he required it still, that the Lord should, when he came for healing, present him with forgiveness. Nor did He follow it at once with the cure of his body, but delayed that for a little, probably for the man's sake, as probably for the sake of those present, whom He had been teaching for some time, and in whose hearts He would now fix the lesson concerning the divine forgiveness which He had preached to them in bestowing it upon the sick man. For His words meant nothing, except they meant that God forgave the man. The scribes were right when they said that none could forgive sins but God — that is, in the full sense in which forgiveness is still needed by every human being, should all his fellows whom he has injured have forgiven him already.

They said in their hearts, "It is blasphemy." This was what He had expected.

"Why do you question in your hearts?" He said, that is, *tnink evil of me — that I am a blasphemer.*

He would now show them that He was no blasphemer, that He had the power to forgive, that it was the will of God that He should preach the remission of sins. How could He show it them? In one way only: by dismissing the consequence, the punishment of those sins, sealing thus in the individual case the general truth. He who could say to a man, by the eternal law that suffering is the consequences of sin: "Be whole, well, strong; suffer no more," must have the right to pronounce his forgiveness; else there was another than God who had to cure with a word the man whom his Maker had afflicted. If there were such another, the kingdom of God must be trembling to its fall, for a stronger had invaded and reversed its decrees. Power does not give the right to pardon, but its possession may prove the right. "Which is easier, to say, 'Your sins are forgiven you,' or to say, 'Rise and walk'?" If only God can do either, He who can do the one must be able to do the other.

"That you may know that the Son of man has authority on earth to forgive sins — rise, take up your bed and go home."

Up rose the man, took up that whereon he had lain, and went away, knowing in himself that his sins *were* forgiven him, for he was able to glorify God.

It seems to me against our Lord's usual custom with the scribes and Pharisees to grant them such proof as this. Certainly, to judge by those recorded, the whole miracle was in aspect and order somewhat unusual. But I think the men here assembled were either better than the most of their class, or in a better mood than common, for St. Luke says of them that the power of the Lord was present to heal them. To such therefore proof might be accorded which was denied to others. That He might heal these learned doctors around Him, He forgave the sins first and then cured the palsy of the man before Him. For their sakes He performed the miracle thus. Then, *like priests, like people;* for where their leaders were listening, the people broke open the roof to get the helpless into His presence.

"They were all amazed and glorified God, saying, 'We never saw anything like this.' They were filled with awe, saying, 'We have seen strange things to-day.' "

And yet Capernaum had to be brought down to hell, and

no man can tell the place where it stood.

Two more cases remain, both related by St. Mark alone.

A Man Deaf and Dumb (Mark 7:31-37)

They brought Him a man partially deaf and dumb. He led him aside from the people. He would be alone with him, that He might come the better into relation with that individuality which, until molten from within, is so hard to touch. Possibly had the man come of himself, this might have been less necessary; but I repeat there must have been in every case reason for the individual treatment in the character and condition of the patient. These were patent only to the healer. In this case the closeness of the personal contact, as in those cases of the blind, is likewise remarkable. "He put His fingers into his ears, and He spat and touched his tongue." Always in present disease, bodily contact—in defects of the senses, sometimes contact of a closer kind. He would generate assured faith in Himself as the healer. But there is another remarkable particular here, which, as far as I can remember, would be alone in its kind but for a fuller development of it at the raising of Lazarus. "And looking up to heaven, He sighed."

What did it mean? What first of all *was* it?

That look, was it not a look up to His own Father? That sigh, was it not the unarticulated prayer to the Father of the man who stood beside Him? But did *He* need to look up as if God was in the sky, seeing that God was in *Him*, in His very deepest, inmost being, in fulness of presence, and receiving conscious response, such as He could not find anywhere else—not from the whole gathered universe? Why should He send a sigh, like a David's dove, to carry the thought of His heart to His Father? The Lord could talk to His Father evermore in the forms of which words are but the shadows; nay, infinitely more, without forms at all, in the thoughts which are the souls of the forms. Why then needs He look up and sigh?

That the man, whose faith was merely beginning, might believe that whatever cure came to him from the hand of the healer, came from the hand of God. Jesus did not care to be believed in as the doer of the deed, save the deed itself were recognized as given Him of the Father. If they saw Him only, and not the Father through Him, there was little gained indeed. The upward look and the sigh were surely the outward expression of the link which bound both the Lord and the man to the Father of all. He would lift the man's heart up to the source of every gift. No cure would be worthy gift without that: it might be an injury.

The Blind Man of Bethsaida (Mark 8:22-26)

The last case is that of the blind man of Bethsaida, whom likewise He led apart, out of the town, and whose dull organs He likewise touched with His spittle. Then comes a difference. The deaf man was at once cured; when He had laid His hands on the blind man, his vision was but half-restored. "He asked him, 'Do you see anything?' And he looked up and said, 'I see men: but they look like trees* walking.' " He could tell they were men and not trees, only by their motion. The Master laid His hands once more upon his eyes, and when he looked up again, he saw every man clearly.

In thus graduating the process, our Lord, I think, drew forth, encouraged, enticed into strength the feeble faith of the man. He brooded over him with His holy presence of love. He gave the faith time to grow. He cared more for his faith than his sight. He let him, as it were, watch Him, feel Him doing it, that he might know and believe. There is in this a peculiar resemblance to the ordinary modes God takes in healing men.

These last miracles are especially full of symbolism and analogy. But in considering any of the miracles, I do not

---

*Could it be translated, "*As well as* (that is besides) trees, I see walkers about"?

care to dwell upon this aspect of them, for in this they are only like all the rest of the doings of God. Nature is brimful of symbolic and analogical parallels to the goings and comings, the growth and the changes of the highest nature in man. It could not be otherwise. For not only did they issue from the same thought, but the one is made for the other. Nature is an outer garment for man, or a living house, rather, for man to live in. So likewise must all the works of Him who did the works of the Father bear the same mark of the original of all.

The one practical lesson contained in this group is nearer the human fact and the human need than any symbolic meaning, grand as it must be, which they may likewise contain. It is that if ever there was a Man such as we read about here, then he who prays for his friends shall be heard of God. I do not say he shall have whatever he asks for. God forbid. But he shall be heard. And the man who does not see the good of that, knows nothing of the good of prayer. He can, I fear, as yet, only pray for himself, when most he fancies he is praying for his friend.

Often, indeed, when men suppose they are concerned for the well-beloved, they are only concerned about what they shall do without them. Let them pray for themselves instead, for that will be the truer prayer. I repeat, all prayer is assuredly heard. The prayer argues a need—that need will be supplied. One day is with the Lord as a thousand years, and a thousand years as one day. All who have prayed shall one day justify God and say, "Your answer is beyond my prayer, as your thoughts and your ways are beyond my thoughts and my ways."

For Thought and Discussion:

1. What do the incidents in this chapter teach concerning the spiritual relations of people one to another in the Body of Christ?

2. Why is the determined exercise of one's own will in prayer a dire evil? How can one avoid it, and still pray specifically and earnestly?

The Official's Son:
1. Why does the human heart cry out for "signs and wonders" to believe? What should the Christian's attitude be towards the so-called "commonplace"?

2. How may parents avoid the error of imposing their spiritual "finding" upon their children's "seeking"?

The Daughter of the Syrophoenician Woman:
1. Explain in your own words, step by step, why Jesus handles this woman as He does.

2. How may we inadvertently fall prey to a spirit of religious exclusiveness? What steps should we take to prevent it?

The Centurion's Servant:
Precisely what were the qualities of the centurion's faith that made Jesus marvel?

The Paralytic:
What particular truths concerning sin, suffering and forgiveness could the witnesses learn from the particular process by which Jesus healed this man?

The Man Deaf and Dumb
What are the implications of Christ's looking heavenward and sighing as He healed this man?

The Blind Man of Bethsaida
What should our responses be when we see our prayers but partially answered?

SEVEN

THE CASTING OUT OF DEVILS

*B*efore attempting to say the little I can concerning this group of miracles, I would protect myself against possible misapprehension. The question concerning the nature of what is called *possession* has nothing whatever to do with that concerning the existence or nonexistence of a personal and conscious power of evil, the one great adversary of the kingdom of heaven, commonly called Satan, or the devil. I say they are two distinct questions, and have so little in common that the one may be argued without even an allusion to the other.

Many think that in the cases recorded we have but the symptoms of well-known diseases, which, from their exceptionally painful character, involving loss of reason, involuntary or convulsive motions, and other abnormal phenomena, the imaginative and unscientific Easterns attributed, as the easiest mode of accounting for them, to a foreign power taking possession of the body and mind of the man. They say there is no occasion whatever to resort to an explanation involving an agency of which we know nothing from any experience of our own. As our Lord did not come to rectify men's psychological or physiological theories, He adopted the mode of speech common among them, but cast out the evil spirits simply by healing the diseases attributed to their influences.

There seems to me nothing unchristian in this interpretation. All diseases that trouble humanity may well be regarded as inroads of the evil powers upon the palaces and temples of God, where only the Holy Spirit has a right to dwell. To cast out such is a marvel altogether as great as to expel the intruding forces to which the Jews attributed some of them. Certainly also our Lord must have used multitudes of human expressions which did not more than adumbrate His own knowledge.

And yet I cannot admit that the solution meets all the appearances of the difficulty. I say *appearances,* because I could not be dogmatic here if I would. I know too little, understand too little, to dare to give such an opinion as possesses even the authority of personal conviction. All I have to say on the subject must therefore come to little. Perhaps if the marvellous, as such, were to me more difficult of belief, anything I might have to say on the side of it would have greater weight. But to me the marvellous is not therefore incredible, always provided that in itself the marvellous thing appears worthy.

I have no difficulty in receiving the old Jewish belief concerning possession, and I think it better explains the phenomena recorded than the growing modern opinion. That a man should rave in madness because some little cell or two in the grey matter of his brain is out of order, is surely no more within the compass of man's understanding than the supposition that an evil spirit, getting close to the fountain of a man's physical life, should disturb all the goings on of that life, even to the production of the most appalling moral phenomena. In either case it is not the man himself who originates the resulting actions, but an external power operating on the man.

There seems to me nothing unreasonable in the supposition of the existence of spirits who, having once had bodies such as ours, and having abused the privileges of embodiment, are condemned for a season to roam about bodiless, ever mourning the loss of their capacity for the only pleasures they care for, and craving after them in their imaginations. Such, either in selfish hate of those who have what they have lost, or from eagerness to come as near the possession of a corporeal form as they may, might well seek to *enter into* a man. The supposition at least is perfectly consistent with the facts recorded. Possibly also it may be consistent with the phenomena of some of the forms of the madness of our own day, although all its forms are alike regarded as resulting from physical causes alone.

The Demoniac at Capernaum (Mark 1:23-27, Luke 4:31-37)

The first act of dispossession recorded is that told by St. Mark and St. Luke, as taking place at Capernaum, amongst His earliest miracles, and preceding the cure of Simon's mother-in-law. He was in the synagogue on the Sabbath day, teaching the congregation, when a man present, who had an unclean spirit, cried out. If I accept the narrative, I find this cry far more intelligible on the old than on the new theory. The speaker, no doubt using the organs of the man, brain and all, for utterance, recognizes a presence—to him the cause of terror—which he addresses as the Holy One of God. This holy one he would propitiate by entreaty and the flattering acknowledgment of His divine mission, with the hope of being left unmolested in the usurpation and cruelty

by which he ministered to his own shadowy self-indul-
gences.

Could anything be more consistently diabolic? What
other word could Jesus address to such than, "Be silent, and
come out of him"? A being in such a condition could not be
permitted to hold converse with the Savior, for he recognized no salvation but what lay in the continuance of his
own pleasures at the expense of another. The form of
rebuke plainly assumes that it was not the man but some one
in the man who had spoken, and the narrative goes on to
say that when the devil had thrown him down and torn him
and cried with a loud voice — his rage and disappointment,
I presume, finding its last futile utterance in the torture of
his captive — he came out of him and left him unhurt.

Thereupon the people questioned amongst themselves
saying, "What is this? A new teaching! With authority He
commands even the unclean spirits, and they obey Him";
thus connecting at once His power over the unclean spirits
with the doctrine He taught, just as our Lord in an after-
instance associates power over demons with spiritual condition. It was the truth in Him that made Him strong against
the powers of untruth.

The Blind and Dumb Demoniac (Matthew 12:22-32; Luke 11:14-23)

Many such cures were performed, but the individual instances recorded are few. The next is that of the man —
dumb, according to St. Luke, both blind and dumb, according to St. Matthew — who spoke and saw as soon as the
devil was cast out of him. With unerring instinct the people
concluded that He who did such deeds must be the Son of
David. The devils themselves, according to St. Mark, were
wont to acknowledge Him the Son of God. The Scribes and
Pharisees, the would-be guides of the people, alone refused
the witness, and in the very imbecility of unbelief, eager
after any theory that might seem to cover the facts without

acknowledging a divine mission in one who would not admit *their* authority, attributed to Beelzebub himself the deliverance of distressed mortals from the powers of evil. Regarding the kingdom of God as a thing of externals, they were fortified against recognizing in Jesus Himself or in His doctrine any sign that He was the enemy of Satan, and might even persuade themselves that such a cure was only one of Satan's tricks for the advancement of his kingdom with the many by a partial emancipation of the individual.

But our Lord attributes this false conclusion to its true cause—to no incapacity or mistake of judgment—but to a preference for any evil which would support them in their authority with the people—in itself an evil. Careless altogether about truth itself, they would not give a moment's quarter to any individual utterance of it which tended to destroy their honorable position in the nation. Each man to himself was his own god. The Spirit of God they shut out.

To them forgiveness was not offered. They must pay the uttermost farthing—whatever that may mean—and frightful as the doom must be. That He spoke thus against them was but a further carrying out of His mission, a further inroad upon the kingdom of that Beelzebub. And yet they were the accredited authorities in the church of that day, and he who does not realize this, does not understand the battle our Lord had to fight for the emancipation of the people. It was for the sake of the people that He called the Pharisees *hypocrites,* and not for their own sakes, for how should He argue with men who taught religion for their own aggrandizement?

It is to be noted that our Lord recognizes the powers of others besides Himself to cast out devils. "By whom do your sons cast them out?" *Did you ever say of them it was by Beelzebub? Why say it of me?* What He claims He freely allows. The Savior had no tinge of that jealousy of rival teaching—as if truth could be two, and could avoid being one—which makes so many of His followers grasp at any waif of false argument. He knew that all good is of God, and not of the devil. All were *with* Him who destroyed the power of the devil.

They who were cured, and they in whom self-worship was not blinding the judgment, had no doubt that He was fighting Satan on his usurped ground. Torture was what might be expected of Satan; healing what might be expected of God. The reality of the healing, the loss of the man, morally as well as physically, to the kingdom of evil, was witnessed in all the signs that followed. Our Lord rests His argument on the fact that Satan had lost these men.

We hear next, from St. Luke, of certain women who followed Him, having been healed of evil spirits and infirmities among whom is mentioned "Mary, called Magdalene, out of whom seven demons had gone out" (Luke 8:2). No wonder a woman thus delivered should devote her restored self to the service of Him who had recreated her. We hear nothing of the circumstances of the cure, only the result in her constant ministration.

Hers is a curious instance of the worthlessness of what some think it a mark of high-mindedness to regard alone —the opinion, namely, of posterity. Without a fragment of evidence, this woman has been all but universally regarded as impure. But what a trifle to her! Down in this squabbling nursery of the race, the name of Mary Magdalene may be degraded even to a subject for pictorial sentimentalities; but the woman herself is with that Jesus who set her free. To the end of time they may call her what they please; to her it is worth but a smile of holy amusement. And just as worthy is the applause of posterity associated with a name. To God we live or die. Let us fall, as, thank Him, we must, into His hands. Let Him judge us. Posterity may be wiser than we; but posterity is not our judge.

The Gadarene Demoniac (Matthew 8:28-34; Mark 5:1-20; Luke 8:26-39)

We now come to a narrative containing more of the marvellous than all the rest. The miracle was wrought on the south-eastern side of the lake — St. Matthew says, upon two demoniacs; St. Mark and St. Luke make mention only of one. The accounts given by the latter Evangelists are much more circumstantial than that by the former. It was a case of peculiarly frightful character. The man, possessed of many demons, was ferocious, and of marvellous strength, breaking chains and fetters, and untameable.

It is impossible to analyze the phenomena, saying which were the actions of the man, and which those of the possessing demons. Externally all were the man's, done by the man finally — some part, I presume, from his own poor withered will, far the greater from the urging of the demons. Even in the case of a man driven by appetite or passion, it is impossible to say how much is to be attributed to the man himself, and how much to that lower nature in him which he ought to keep in subjection, but which, having been allowed to get the upper hand, has become a possessing demon.

He met the Lord worshipping, and, as in a former instance, praying for such clemency as devils can value. Was it the devils, then, that urged the man into the presence of the Lord? Was it not rather the other spirit, the spirit of life, which not the presence of a legion of the wicked ones could drive from him? Was it not the spirit of the Father in him which brought him, ignorant, fearing, yet vaguely hoping perhaps, to the feet of the Son? He knew not why he came; but he came — drawn or driven; he could not keep away.

When he came, however, the words at least of his prayer were molded by the devils — "I adjure you by God, do not torment me." Think of the man, tortured by such awful presences, praying to the healer not to torment him! The prayer was compelled into this shape by the indwelling demons. They would have him pray for indulgence for them. But the Lord heard the deeper prayer, that is, the need and misery of the man — the horror that made him cry and cut himself with stones — and commanded the unclean spirit to come out of him.

Thereupon, St. Mark says, "he begged Him eagerly not to send them out of the country." Probably the country was one the condition of whose inhabitants afforded the demons unusual opportunities for their coveted pseudo-embodiment. St. Luke says, "They begged Him not to command them to depart into the abyss" — to such beings awful, chiefly because there they must be alone, afar from matter and all its forms. In such loneliness the good man would be filled with the eternal presence of the living God, but they would be aware only of their greedy, hungry selves — desires without objects.

No. Here were swine. "Send us to the swine, let us enter them." Deprived of the abode they preferred, debarred from men, swine would serve their turn. But even the swine — animals created to look unclean, for a type to humanity of the very form and fashion of its greed — could not endure their presence. The man had cut himself with stones in his misery; the swine in theirs rushed into the waters of the lake and were drowned. The evil spirits, I presume, having no further leave, had to go to their deep after all.

The destruction of the swine must not be regarded as miraculous. But there must have been a special reason in the character and condition of the people of Gadara for His allowing this destruction of their property. I suppose that although it worked vexation and dismay at first, it prepared the way for some after-reception of the gospel. Now, seeing him who had been a raving maniac, sitting at the feet of Jesus, clothed and in his right mind, and hearing what had come to the swine, they were filled with fear, and prayed the healer to depart from them.

But who can imagine the delight of the man when that wild troop of maddening and defiling demons, which had possessed him with all uncleanness, vanished! Scarce had he time to know that he was naked, before the hands of loving human beings, in whom the good Spirit ruled, were taking off their own garments and putting them upon him. He was a man once more, and among men with human faces, human hearts, human ways. He was with his own, and that supreme form and face of the man who had set him free was binding them all into one holy family.

Now he could pray of himself the true prayer of a soul which knew what it wanted, and could say what it meant. He sat down like a child at the feet of the man who had cured him. When, yielding at once to the desire of those who would be rid of his presence, Jesus went down to the boat, he followed, praying that he might be with Him. What could he desire but to be near that power which had restored him his divine self, and the consciousness thereof — his own true existence, that of which God was thinking when He made him?

But he would be still nearer the Lord in doing His work than in following Him about. It is remarkable that while more than once our Lord charged the healed to be silent, He leaves this man as his apostle — his witness with those who had banished Him from their coasts. Something may be attributed to the different natures of the individuals; some in preaching Him would also preach themselves, and so hurt both. But this man was not of such. To be with the Lord was all his prayer. Therefore he was fit to be without Him, and to aid His work apart.

But I think it more likely that the reason lay in the condition of the people. Judaea was in a state of excitement about Him — that excitement had unhealthy elements, and must not be fanned. In some places the Lord would not speak at all. Through some He would pass unknown. But here all was different. He had destroyed their swine; they had prayed Him to depart. If He took from them this one sign of His real presence, that is, of the love which heals, not the power which destroys it, it would be to abandon them.

But it is very noteworthy that He sent the man to his own house, to his own friends. They must be the most open to such a message as his, and from such lips — the lips of their own flesh and blood. He had been raving in tombs and deserts, tormented with a legion of devils. Now he was one of themselves again, with love in his eyes, adoration in the very tones of his voice, and help in his hands — reason once more supreme on the throne of humanity. He obeyed, and published in Gadara, and the rest of the cities of Decapolis, the great things, as Jesus Himself called them, which God had done for him. For it was God who had done them. He was doing the works of his Father.

One more instance remains, having likewise peculiar points of difficulty, and therefore of interest.

The Lunatic Boy (Matthew 17:14-20; Mark 9:14-29; Luke 9:37-43)

When Jesus was on the mount of transfiguration, a dumb, epileptic, and lunatic boy was brought by his father to those disciples who were awaiting His return. But they could do nothing. To their disappointment, and probably to their chagrin, they found themselves powerless over the evil spirit. When Jesus appeared, the father begged of Him the aid which His disciples could not give: "Teacher, I beg you to look upon my son, for he is my only child."

Whoever has held in his arms his child in delirium, calling to his father for aid as if he were distant far, and beating the air in wild and aimless defense, will be able to enter a little into the trouble of this man's soul. To have the child, and yet find himself with a great abyss between him and his child, across which the cry of the child comes, but back across which no answering voice can reach the consciousness of the sufferer — is terror and misery indeed.

But imagine in the case before us the intervals as well — the stupidity, the vacant gaze, the hanging lip, the pale flaccid countenance and bloodshot eyes, idiocy alternated with madness—no voice of human speech, only the animal babble of the uneducated dumb—the misery of his falling down anywhere, now in the fire, now in the water, and the divine shines out as nowhere else—for the father loves his only child even to agony. What was there in such a child to love? *Everything:* the human was there, else whence the torture of that which was not human? God was there. The misery was that the devil was there too. Thence came the crying and tears. "Rescue the divine; send the devil to the deep," was the unformed prayer in the father's soul.

Before replying to his prayer, Jesus uttered words that could not have been addressed to the father, inasmuch as he was neither faithless nor perverse. Which then of those present did He address thus? To which of them did He say, "How long am I to be with you? How long am I to bear with you?" I have thought it was the bystanders: but why they? They had not surely reached the point of such rebuke. I have thought it was the disciples, because perhaps it was their pride that rendered them unable to cast out the demon, seeing they tried it without faith enough in God. But the form of address does not seem to belong to them. The word *generation* could not well apply to those whom He had chosen out of that generation.

I have thought, and gladly would I continue to think, if I could honestly, that the words were intended for the devils who tormented his countrymen and friends; and but for St. Mark's story, I might have held to it. He, however, gives us one point which neither St. Matthew nor St. Luke mention—that "when they came to the disciples, they saw a great crowd about them, and scribes arguing with them." He says the multitude were greatly amazed when they saw Him—why, I do not know, except it be that He came just at the point where His presence was needful to give the one answer to the scribes pressing hard upon His disciples because they could not cast out this devil. These scribes, these men of accredited education, who, from their position as students of the law and the interpretations thereof, arrogated to themselves a mastery over the faith of the people, but were themselves so careless about the truth as to be utterly opaque to its illuminating power. I do think it was these scribes whom our Lord addressed as "faithless and perverse generation." The immediately following request to the father of the boy, "Bring him here to me," was the one answer to their arguments.

A fresh paroxysm was the first result. But repressing all haste, the Lord will care for the father as much as for the child. He will help his growing faith.

"How long has he had this?"

"From childhood. And it has often cast him into the fire and into the water to destroy him; but if you can do anything, have pity on us and help us."*

"*If you can?* All things are possible to him who believes."

"I believe; help my unbelief."

Whether the words of Jesus, "him who believes," meant Himself as believing in the Father, and therefore gifted with all power, or the man as believing in Him, and therefore capable of being the recipient of the effects of that power, I am not sure. I incline to the former. The result is the same, for the man resolves the question practically and personally. What was needful in him should be in him. "I believe; help my unbelief."

In the honesty of his heart, lest he should be saying more than was true—for how could he be certain that Jesus would cure his son? or how could he measure and estimate his own faith?—he appeals to the Lord of Truth for all that he ought to be, and think, and believe. "Help my unbelief." It is the very triumph of faith. The unbelief itself cast like any other care upon Him who cares for us, is the highest exercise of belief. It is the greatest effort lying in the power of the man.

---

*Again the *us*—so full of pathos.

No man can help doubt. The true man alone, that is, the faithful man, can appeal to the Truth to enable him to believe what is true, and refuse what is false. How this applies especially to our own time and the need of the living generations, is easy to see. Of all prayers it is the one for us.

Possibly our Lord might have held a little farther talk with him, but the people came crowding about. "He rebuked the unclean spirit, saying to it, 'You dumb and deaf spirit, I command you, come out of him, and never enter him again.' And after crying out and convulsing him terribly, it came out, and the boy was like a corpse; so that most of them said, 'He is dead.' But Jesus took him by the hand and lifted him up, and he arose."

"Why could we not cast it out?" asked his disciples as soon as they were alone.

"This kind cannot be driven out by anything but prayer" ["and fasting"; see note, RSV. Ed.].

What does this answer imply? The prayer and fasting must clearly be on the part of those who would heal. They cannot be required of one possessed with a demon. If he could fast and pray, the demon would be gone already.

It implies that a great purity of soul is needful in him who would master the powers of evil. I take the prayer and fasting to indicate a condition of mind elevated above the cares of the world and the pleasures of the senses, in close communion with the God of life; therefore by its very purity it is an awe and terror to the unclean spirits, a fit cloud whence the thunder of the word might issue against them. The expulsion would appear to be the result of moral, and hence natural, superiority. It would result from a common resting upon oneness with the ultimate will of the Supreme, in like manner as an evil man is sometimes cowed in the presence of a good man. The disciples had not attained this lofty condition of faith.

From this I lean to think that the words of our Lord— "All things are possible to him who believes"—apply to our

Lord Himself. The disciples could not help the child. "If you can do anything," said the father. "All things are possible to him who believes," says our Lord. *He* can help him. That it was the lack of faith in the disciples which rendered the thing impossible for them, St. Matthew informs us explicitly, for he gives the reply of our Lord more fully than the rest: "Because of your little faith," He said, and followed with the assertion that faith could remove mountains.

But the words — *"This kind"* — suggest that the case had its peculiarities. It would appear — although I am not certain of this interpretation — that some kinds of spirits required for their expulsion, or at least some cases of possession required for their cure, more than others of the presence of God in the healer. I do not care to dwell upon this farther than to say that there are points in the narrative which seem to indicate that it was an unusually bad case. The Lord asked how long he had been ill, and was told, from childhood. The demon — to use the language of our ignorance — had had time and opportunity, in his undeveloped condition, to lay thorough hold upon him. When he did yield to the superior command of the Lord, he left him as dead.

So close had been the possession, that for a time the natural powers could not operate when deprived of the presence of a force which had so long usurped, maltreated, and exhausted, while falsely sustaining them. The disciples, although they had already the power to cast out demons, could not cast this one out, and were surprised to find it so. There appears to me no absurdity, if we admit the demons at all, in admitting also that some had greater force than others, be it regarded as courage or obstinacy, or merely as grasp upon the captive mortal.

In all these stories there is much of comfort both to the friends of those who are insane, and to those who are themselves aware of their own partial or occasional insanity. For such sorrow as that of Charles and Mary Lamb, walking together towards the asylum, when the hour had come for her to repair thither, is there not some assuagement here? It may be answered — We have no ground to hope for such cure now. I think we have; but if our faith will not reach so far, we may at least, like Athanasius, recognize the friendship of Death, for death is the divine cure of many ills.

But we all need like healing. No man who does not yet love the truth with his whole being, who does not love God with all his heart and soul and strength and mind, and his neighbor as himself, is in his sound mind, or can act as a rational being, save more or less approximately. This is as true as it would be of us if possessed by other spirits than our own.

Every word of unkindness, God help us! every unfair hard judgment, every trembling regard of the outward and fearless disregard of the inward life, is a siding with the spirit of evil against the spirit of good, with our lower and accidental selves, against our higher and essential — our true selves. These the Spirit of Good would set free from all possession but His own, for that is their original life. Out of us, too, the evil spirits can go by that prayer alone in which a man draws nigh to the Holy. Nor can we have any power over the evil spirit in others except in proportion as by such prayer we cast the evil spirit out of ourselves.

For Thought and Discussion

1. What are the common outward expressions that demon possession makes in these recorded instances? What are the reasons for MacDonald's accepting these cases as indeed incidents of diabolic manifestations and not simply of pathological disorders?

2. What evils may issue when people in positions of leadership are motivated, like the Pharisees, by strong opinions of their own worth and authority?

3. What are the possible reasons why Jesus bid the Gadarene demoniac not go with Him but stay and witness to his family and friends?

4. What are the implications of the father's cry, "I believe; help my unbelief"? How is it an apt cry for each Christian?

EIGHT

THE RAISING OF THE DEAD

I linger on the threshold. How shall I enter the temple of this wonder? Through all ages men of all degrees and forms of religion have hoped at least for a continuance of life beyond its seeming extinction. Without such a hope, how could they have endured the existence they had?

True, there are in our day men who profess unbelief in that future, and yet lead an enjoyable life, nor even say to themselves, "Let us eat and drink, for tomorrow we die"; but say instead, with nobleness, "Let us do what good we may, for there are men to come after us." Of all things let him who would be a Christian be fair to every man and every class of men. Before, however, I could be satisfied that I understood the mental condition of such, I should require a deeper insight than I possess in respect of other men.

These, however numerous they seem in our day, would appear to be exceptions to the race. No doubt there have always been those who from absorption in the present and its pleasures, have not cared about the future, have not troubled themselves with the thought of it. Some of them would rather not think of it, because if there be such a future, they cannot be easy concerning their part in it. Others are simply occupied with the poor present—a present grand indeed if it be the part of an endless whole, but poor indeed if it stand alone.

But here are thoughtful men, who say, "There is no more. Let us make the best of this." Nor is their notion of *best* contemptible, although in the eyes of some of us, to whom the only worth of being lies in the hope of becoming that which, at the rate of present progress, must take ages to be realized, it is poor. I will venture one or two words on the matter.

Their ideal does not approach the ideal of Christianity for *this* life even.

Before I can tell whether their words are a true representation of themselves, in relation to this future, I must know both their conscious and unconscious being. No wonder I should be loath to judge them.

No poet of high rank, as far as I know, ever disbelieved in the future. He might fear that there was none; but that very fear is faith. The greatest poet of the present day [Browning?—ed.] believes with ardor. That it is not proven to the intellect, I heartily admit. But if it were true, it were such as the intellect could not grasp, for the understanding must be the offspring of the life—in itself essential. How should the intellect understand its own origin and nature? It is too poor to grasp this question; for the continuity of existence depends on the nature of existence, not upon external relations.

If after death we should be conscious that we yet live, we shall even then, I think, be no more able to prove a further continuance of life, than we can now prove our present being. It may be easier to believe — that will be all. But we constantly act upon grounds which we cannot prove, and if we cannot feel so sure of life beyond the grave as of common every-day things, at least the want of proof ought neither to destroy our hope concerning it, nor prevent the action demanded by its bare possibility.

But last, I do say this, that those men, who, disbelieving in a future state, do yet live up to the conscience within them, however much lower the requirements of that conscience may be than those of a conscience which believes itself enlightened from "the Lord, who is that spirit," shall enter the other life in an immeasurably more enviable relation thereto than those who say *Lord, Lord,* and do not the things He says to them.

It may seem strange that our Lord says so little about the life to come, as we call it — though in truth it is one life with the present, as the leaf and the blossom are one life. Even in argument with the Sadducees He supports His side upon words accepted by them, and upon the nature of God, but says nothing of the question from a human point of regard. He seems always to have taken it for granted, ever turning the minds of His scholars towards that which was deeper and lay at its root — the life itself — the oneness with God and His will, upon which the continuance of our conscious being follows of a necessity, and without which if the latter were possible, it would be for human beings an utter evil.

When He speaks of the world beyond, it is as *His Father's house.* He says there are many mansions there. He attempts in no way to explain. Man's own imagination enlightened of the spirit of truth, and working with his experience and affections, was a far safer guide than his intellect with the best schooling even our Lord could have given it. The memory of the poorest home of a fisherman on the shore of the Galilean lake, where He as a child had spent His years of divine carelessness in His father's house, would, at the words of our Lord *my Father's house,* convey to Peter or James or John more truth concerning the many mansions than a revelation to their intellect, had it been possible, as clear as the Apocalypse itself is obscure.

When He said "I have overcome *the world,*" He had overcome the cause of all doubt, the belief in the outside appearances and not in the living truth. He left it to His followers to say, from their own experience knowing the thing, not merely from the belief of His resurrection, "He has conquered death and the grave." "O death, where is thy victory? O death, where is thy sting?" It is the inward life of truth that conquers the outward death of appearance; and nothing else, no revelation from without, could conquer it.

These miracles of our Lord are the nearest we come to news of any kind concerning — I cannot say *from* — the other world. I except of course our Lord's own resurrection. Of that I shall yet speak as a miracle, for miracle it was, as certainly as any of our Lord's whatever interpretation be put upon the word. And I say *the nearest to news we come,* because not one of those raised from the dead gives *us* at least an atom of information. Is it possible they may have told their friends something which has filtered down to us in any shape?

I turn to the cases on record. They are only three.

The Raising of the Widow's Son (Luke 7:11-17)

The day after He cured the servant of the centurion at Capernaum, Jesus went to Nain, and as they approached the gate — but I cannot part the story from the lovely words in which it is told by St. Luke: "Behold, a man who had died was being carried out, the only son of his mother, and she was a widow; and a large crowd from the city was with her. And when the Lord saw her, He had compassion on her and said unto her, 'Do not weep.' And He came and touched the bier; and the bearers stood still. And He said, 'Young man, I say to you, arise.' And the dead man sat up and began to speak. And He gave him to his mother."

In each of the cases there is an especial fitness in the miracle. This youth was the only son of a widow; the daughter of Jairus was "his only daughter"; Lazarus was the brother of two orphan sisters.

I will not attempt by any lingering over the simple details to render the record more impressive. That lingering ought to be on the part of the reader of the narrative itself. Friends crowded around the weeping mother—the dead man borne in the midst. They were going to the house of death, but Life was between them and it—and walking to meet them, although they knew it not. A face of tender pity looks down on the mother. She heeds him not. He goes up to the bier, and lays his hand on it. The bearers recognize authority, and stand. A word, and the dead sits up. A moment more, and he is in the arms of his mother.

O mother! mother! Were you more favored than other mothers? Or was it that, for the sake of all mothers as well as yourself, you were made the type of the universal mother with the dead son—the raising of him but a foretaste of the one universal bliss of mothers with dead sons? That you were an exception would have ill met your need, for your motherhood could not be justified in yourself alone. It could not have its rights save on grounds universal. Your motherhood was common to all your sisters. You were indeed a chosen one, but that you might show to all the last fate of the mourning mother; for in God's dealings there are no exceptions. His laws are universal as He is infinite.

Jesus wrought no new thing—only the works of the Father. What matters it that the dead come not back to us, if we go to them? *What matters it?* I said! It is tenfold better. Dear as home is, he who loves it best must know that what he calls home is not home, is but a shadow of home, is but the open porch of home, where all the winds of the world rave by turns, and the glowing fire of the true home casts lovely gleams from within.

Certainly this mother did not thus lose her son again. Doubtless next she died first, knowing then at last that she had only to wait. The dead must have their sorrow too, but when they find it is well with them, they can sit and wait by the mouth of the coming stream better than those can wait who see the going stream bear their loves down to the ocean of the unknown. The dead sit by the river-mouths of Time: the living mourn upon its higher banks.

But for the joy of the mother, we cannot conceive it. No mother even who has lost her son, and hopes one blessed eternal day to find him again, can conceive her gladness. Had it been all a dream? A dream surely in this sense, that the *final,* which alone, in the full sense, is God's will, must ever cast the look of a dream over all that has gone before. When we last awake we shall know that we dreamed. Even every honest judgment, feeling, hope, desire, will show itself a dream — with this difference from some dreams, that the waking is the more lovely, that nothing is lost, but everything gained, in the full blaze of restored completeness. How triumphant would this mother die, when her turn came! And how calmly would the restored son go about the duties of the world.*

He sat up and began to speak.

It is vain to look into that which God has hidden; for surely it is by no chance that we are left thus in the dark. "He began to speak." Why does not the Evangelist go on to give us some hint of what he said? Would not the hearts of [all concerned] have blessed God for St. Luke's record of what the son of the widow said? For my part, I thank God he was silent. When I think of the pictures of heaven drawn from the attempt of prophecy to utter its visions in the poor

---

*Those who can take the trouble, and are capable of understanding it, will do well to study Robert Browning's "Epistle to an Arab Physician."

forms of the glory of earth, I see it better that we should walk by faith, and not by a fancied sight.

I judge that the region beyond is so different from ours, so comprising in one surpassing excellence all the goods of ours, that any attempt of the had-been-dead to describe it would have resulted in the most wretched of misconceptions. Such might please the lower conditions of Christian development—but so much the worse, for they could not fail to obstruct its further growth. It is well that St. Luke is silent; or that the mother and the friends who stood by the bier, heard the words of the returning spirit only as the babble of a child from which they could draw no definite meaning, and to which they could respond only by caresses.

The Raising of the Daughter of Jairus (Matthew 9:18-26; Mark 5:35-43; Luke 8:49-56)

The story of the daughter of Jairus is recorded briefly by St. Matthew, more fully by St. Luke, most fully by St. Mark. One of the rulers of the synagogue at Capernaum falls at the feet of our Lord, saying his little daughter is at the point of death. She was about twelve years of age. He begs the Lord to lay His hands on her that she may live. Our Lord goes with him, followed by many people. On His way to restore the child He is arrested by a touch. He makes no haste to outstrip death. We can imagine the impatience of the father when the Lord stood and asked who touched Him. What did that matter? His daughter was dying. Death would not wait. But the woman's heart and soul must not be passed by. The father with the only daughter must wait yet a little. The will of God cannot be outstripped.

"While He was still speaking, there came from the ruler's house some who said, 'Your daughter is dead: why trouble the Teacher any further?'" "Ah! I thought so! There it is! Death has won the race!" we may suppose the father to say —bitterly within himself. But Jesus, while He tried the faith of men, never tried it without feeding its strength. With the trial He always gives a way of escape. "But ignoring what they said"—not leaving it to work its agony of despair first—"Jesus said to the ruler of the synagogue, 'Do not fear; only believe.' " They are such simple words—commonplace in the ears of those who have heard them often and heeded them little! But they contain more for this man's peace than all the consolations of philosophy, than all the enforcements of morality; yea, even than the raising of his daughter itself.

To arouse the higher, the hopeful, the trusting nature of a man; to cause him to look up into the unknown region of mysterious possibilities—to the God so poorly known—is to do infinitely more for a man than to remove the pressure of the direst evil without it. I will go further: To arouse the hope that there may be a God with a heart like our own is more for the humanity in us than to produce the absolute conviction that there is a being who made the heaven and the earth and the sea and the fountains of waters. Jesus is the express image of God's substance, and in Him we know the heart of God. To nourish faith in Himself was the best thing He could do for the man.

Now it would appear that He stopped the crowd and would let them go no farther. They could not all see, and He did not wish them to see. It was not good for men to see too many miracles. They would feast their eyes, and then cease to wonder or think. The miracle, which would be all, and quite dissociated from religion, with many of them, would cease to be wonderful, would become a common thing with most. Yea, some would cease to believe that it had been. They would say she did sleep after all—she was not dead. A wonder is a poor thing for faith after all. The miracle could be only a wonder in the eyes of those who had not prayed for it, and could not give thanks for it; who did not feel that in it they were partakers of the love of God.

Jesus *must* have hated anything like display. God's greatest work has never been done in crowds, but in closets; and when it works out from thence, it is not upon crowds, but upon individuals. A crowd is not a divine thing. It is not a body. Its atoms are not members one of another. A crowd is a chaos over which the Spirit of God has yet to move, ere each retires to his place to begin his harmonious work, and unite with all the rest in the organized chorus of the human creation. The crowd must be dispersed that the church may be formed.

The relation of the crowd to the miracle is rightly reflected in what came to the friends of the house. To them, weeping and wailing greatly, after the Eastern fashion, He said when He entered, "Why do you make a tumult and weep? The child is not dead but sleeping." They laughed Him to scorn. He put them all out.

But what did our Lord mean by those words—"The child is not dead but sleeping"? Not certainly that, as we regard the difference between death and sleep, His words were to be taken literally; not that she was only in a state of coma or lethargy; not even that it was a case of suspended animation as in catalepsy; for the whole narrative evidently intends us to believe that she was dead after the fashion we call death. That this was not to be dead after the fashion our Lord called death, is a blessed and lovely fact.

Neither can it mean, that she was not dead as others, in that He was going to wake her so soon. For they did not know that, and therefore it could give no ground for the expostulation, "Why do you make a tumult and weep?"

Nor yet could it come *only* from the fact that to His eyes death and sleep were so alike, the one needing the power of God for awaking just as much as the other. True, they must be more alike in His eyes than even in the eyes of the many poets who have written of "Death and his brother Sleep." But He sees the differences none the less clearly, and how they look to us, and His knowledge could be no reason for reproaching our ignorance.

The explanation seems to me large and simple. These

people professed to believe in the resurrection of the dead, and did believe after some feeble fashion. They were not Sadducees, for they were the friends of a ruler of the synagogue. Our Lord did not bring the news of resurrection to the world. That had been believed, in varying degrees, by all peoples and nations from the first. The resurrection He taught was a far deeper thing—the resurrection from dead works to serve the living and true God. But as with the greater number even of Christians, although it was part of their creed, and had some influence upon their moral and spiritual condition, their practical faith in the resurrection of the body was a poor affair. In the moment of loss and grief, they thought little about it. They lived then in the present almost alone; they were not saved by hope.

The reproach therefore of our Lord was simply that they did not take from their own creed the consolation they ought. If the child was to be one day restored to them, then she was not dead *as* their tears and lamentations would imply. Any one of themselves who believed in God and the prophets, might have stood up and said—"Foolish mourners, why make such commotion? The maid is not dead, but sleeps. You shall again clasp her to your bosom. Hope, and fear not—only believe." It was in this sense, I think, that our Lord spoke.

But it may not at first appear how much grander the miracle itself appears in the light of this simple interpretation of the Master's words. The sequel stands in the same relation to the words as if—turning into the death-chamber, and bringing the girl out by the hand—He had said to them: "See—I told you she was not dead but sleeping." The words apply to all death, just as much as to that in which this girl lay. The Lord brings His assurance, His knowledge of what we do not know, to feed our feeble faith.

It is as if He told us that our notion of death is all wrong, that there is no such thing as we think it; that we should be nearer the truth if we denied it altogether, and gave to what we now call death the name of sleep, for it is but a passing appearance, and no right cause of such misery as we manifest in its presence.

I think it was from this word of our Lord, and from the same utterance in the case of Lazarus, that St. Paul so often uses the word *sleep* for *die* and for *death*. Indeed the notion of death, as we feel it, seems to have vanished entirely from St. Paul's mind—he speaks of things so in a continuity, not even referring to the change—not even saying *before death* or *after death,* as if death made no atom of difference in the progress of holy events, the divine history of the individual and of the race together. In a word, when He raised the dead, the Son did neither more nor less nor other than the work of the Father—what He is always doing. He only made it manifest a little sooner to the eyes and hearts of men.

But they to whom He spoke laughed Him to scorn. They knew she was dead, and their unfaithfulness blinded their hearts to what He meant. They were unfit to behold the proof of what He had said. Such as they, in such mood, could gather from it no benefit. A faithful heart alone is capable of understanding the proof of the truest things. It is faith towards God which alone can lay hold of any of His facts.

There is a foregoing fitness. Therefore He put them all out. But the father and mother, whose love and sorrow made them more easily persuaded of mighty things, more accessible to holy influences, and the three disciples, whose faith rendered them fit to behold otherwise dangerous wonders, He took with Him into the chamber where the girl lay—dead toward men—sleeping toward God. Dead as she was, she only slept.

"Little girl, I say to you, arise." "And her spirit returned," "and immediately the girl got up and walked," "and He directed that something should be given her to eat." For in the joy of her restoration, they might forget that the more complete the health of a worn and exhausted body, the more needful was food. Food, in all its commonness, might well support the miracle; for not only did it follow by the next word to that which had wrought the miracle, but it worked in perfect harmony with the law which took shape in this resurrection, and in its relations to the human being involved no less marvel than lay in the miracle itself. The raising of the dead and the feeding of the living are both and equally divine—therefore in utter harmony.

And we do not any more understand the power in the body which takes to itself that food, than we understand the power going out from Jesus to make this girl's body capable of again employing its ministrations. They are both of one and must be perfect in harmony, the one as much the outcome of law as the other.

He charges the parents to be silent, it may be for His sake, who did not want to be made a mere wonder of, but more probably for their sakes, that the holy thing might not evaporate in speech, or be defiled with foolish talk and the glorification of self-importance in those for whom a mighty wonder had been done. In silence the seed might take root in their hearts and bring forth living fruit in humility, and uprightness, and faith.

The Raising of Lazarus (John 11:1-54)

And now for the wonderful story of Lazarus. In this miracle one might think the desire of Jesus for His friend's presence through His own coming trouble, might have had a share, were it not that we never find Him working a miracle for Himself. He knew the perfect will of the Father, and left all to Him. Those who cannot know that will and do not care for it, have to fall into trouble that they may know God as the Savior from their own doings—as the fountain of all their well-being. This Jesus had not to learn, and therefore could need no miracle wrought for Him. Even His resurrection was all for others. The miracle was wrought in Him, not for Him.

He knew Lazarus was dying. He abode where He was and let him die. For a hard and therefore precious lesson for sisters and friends lay in that death, and the more the love the more precious the lesson — the same that lies in every death; and the end the same for all who love — resurrection. The raising of Lazarus is the type of the raising of all the dead. Of Lazarus, as of the daughter of Jairus, He said he "has fallen asleep, but I go to awake him out of sleep." He slept as every dead man sleeps.

Read the story. Try to think not only what the disciples felt, but what Jesus was thinking; how He, who saw the other side, regarded the death He was about to destroy.

"Lord, if you had been here," said Martha, "my brother would not have died."

Did she mean to hint what she had not faith enough to ask?

"Your brother will rise again," said the Lord.

But her faith was so weak that she took little comfort from the assurance. Alas! she knew what it meant. She knew all about it. He spoke of the general far-off resurrection, which to her was a very little thing. It was true he should rise again; but what was that to the present consuming grief? A thousand years might be to God as one day, but to Martha the one day was a thousand years. It is only to him who entirely believes in God that the thousand years become one day also. For he that believes shares in the vision of Him in whom He believes.

It is through such faith that Jesus would help her — far beyond the present awful need. He seeks to raise her confidence in Himself by the strongest assertions of the might that was in Him. "I am the resurrection and the life: he who believes in me, though he die, yet shall he live!" The death of not believing in God — the God revealed in Jesus — is the only death. The other is nowhere but in the fears and fancies of unbelief. "And whoever lives and believes in me shall never die." There is for him nothing to be called death;

nothing that is what death *looks* to us.

"Do you believe this?"

Martha was an honest woman. She did not fully understand what He meant. She could not, therefore, do more than assent to it. But she believed in *Him,* and that much she could tell Him plainly.

"Yes, Lord; I believe that you are the Christ, the Son of God, He who is coming into the world."

And, that hope with the confession having arisen in her heart, she gave the loveliest sign. She went and called her sister. But even in the profounder Mary faith reached only to the words of her sister:

"Lord, if you had been here, my brother would not have died."

When He saw her trouble, and that of the Jews with her, He was troubled likewise. But why? The purest sympathy with what was about to vanish would not surely make Him groan in His spirit. Why, then, this trouble in our Lord's heart? We have a right, yes, a duty, to understand it if we can, for He showed it.

I think it was caused by an invading sense of the general misery of poor humanity from the lack of that faith in the Father without which He, the Son, could do, or endure, nothing. If the Father ceased the Son must cease. It was the darkness between God and His creatures that gave room for and was filled with their weeping and wailing over their dead. To them death must appear an unmitigated and irremediable evil.

How frightful to feel as they felt! to see death as they saw it! Nothing could help their misery but that faith in the infinite love which He had come to bring them. But how hard it was to persuade them to receive it! And how many weeping generations of loving hearts must follow! His Father was indeed with them all, but how slowly and painfully would each learn the one precious fact!

"Where have you laid him?" He asked.

"Lord, come and see," they answered, in such mournful accents of human misery that He wept with them.

They come to the grave.

"Take away the stone."

"Lord, by this time there will be an odor, for he has been dead four days," said she who believed in the Resurrection and the Life! They are the saddest of sad words. I hardly know how to utter the feeling they raise. In all the relations of mortality to immortality, of body to soul, there are painful and even ugly things, things to which, by common consent, we refer only upon dire necessity, and with a sense of shame. Happy they in whom the mortal has put on immortality!

Decay and its accompaniments, all that makes the most beloved of the *appearances* of God's creation a terror, compelling us to call to the earth for succour, and pray her to take our dead out of our sight, to receive her own back into her bosom, and to unmake in secret darkness that which was the glory of the light in our eyes—this was uppermost with Martha, even in the presence of Him to whom Death was but a slave to come and go at His will. Careful of His feelings, of the shock to His senses, she would oppose His will. For the dead brother's sake also, that he should not be dishonored in his privacy, she would not have had that stone removed. But had it been as Martha feared, who so tender with feeble flesh as the Son of Man? Who so unready to impute the shame it could not help? Who less fastidious over the painful working of the laws of His own world?

Entire affection hateth nicer hands.

And at the worst, what was decay to Him, who could recall the disuniting atoms under the restored law of imperial life?

"Did I not tell you that if you would believe you would see the glory of God?"

Again I say *the essential* glory of God who raises all the dead, not merely *an exceptional* glory of God in raising this one dead man.

They should see not corruption but glory. No evil odor of dissolution should assail them, but glowing life should spring from the place of the dead. Light should be born from the very bosom of the darkness.

They took away the friendly stone. Then Jesus spoke, not to the dead man, but to the living Father. The men and women about Him must know it as the Father's work. "And Jesus lifted up His eyes and said, Father, I thank thee that thou hast heard me. I know that thou hearest me always, but I have said this on account of the people standing by, that they may believe that thou didst send me." So might they believe that the work was God's, that He was doing the will of God, and that they might trust in the God whose will was such as this. He claimed the presence of God in what He did, that by the open claim and the mighty deed following it they might see that the Father justified what the Son said, and might receive Him and all that He did as the manifestation of the Father. And now —

"Lazarus, come out."

Slow toiling, with hand and foot bound in the grave clothes, he that had been dead struggled forth to the light. What an awful moment! When did ever corruption and glory meet and embrace as now! Oh! what ready hands, eager almost to helplessness, were stretched trembling towards the feeble man returning from his strange journey, to seize and carry him into the day — their poor day, which they thought *all* the day. They were forgetful of that higher day which for their sakes he had left behind, content to walk in moonlight a little longer, gladdened by the embraces of his sisters, and — perhaps — I do not know — comforting their hearts with news of the heavenly regions!

Joy of all joys! The dead come back! Is it any wonder that this Mary should spend three hundred pence on an ointment for the feet of the Raiser of the Dead?

I doubt if he told them anything. I do not think he could make even his own flesh and blood—of womankind, quick to understand—know the things he had seen and heard and felt. All that can be said concerning this, is thus said by our beloved brother Tennyson in his book *In Memoriam:*

'Where wert thou, brother, those four days?'
    There lives no record of reply,
    Which telling what it is to die,
Had surely added praise to praise.

Behold a man raised up by Christ!
    The rest remaineth unrevealed;
    He told it not; or something sealed
The lips of that Evangelist.

Why are we left in such ignorance?

Without the raising of the dead, without the rising of the Savior Himself, Christianity would not have given what it could of *hope* for the future. Hope is not faith, but neither is faith sight; and if we have hope we are not miserable men. But Christianity must not, could not interfere with the discipline needful for its own fulfillment, could not depose the schoolmaster that leads unto Christ. One main doubt and terror which drives men towards the revelation in Jesus, is this strange thing Death.

How shall any man imagine he is complete in himself, and can do without a Father in heaven, when he knows that he knows neither the mystery whence he sprung by birth, nor the mystery to which he goes by death? God has given us room away from Himself as Robert Browning says:

... "God, whose pleasure brought
Man into being, stands away,
As it were, an hand-breadth off, to give

Room for the newly-made to live,
And look at Him from a place apart,
And use His gifts of brain and heart" —

and this room, in its time-symbol, is bounded by darkness on the one hand, and darkness on the other. Whence I came and whither I go are dark; how can I live in peace without the God who ordered it thus?

Faith is my only refuge — an absolute belief in a being so much beyond myself, that He can do all for this *me* with utter satisfaction to this *me*, protecting all its rights, jealously as His own from which they spring, that He may make me at last one with Himself who is my deeper self, inasmuch as His thought of me is my life. And not to know Him, even if I could go on living and happy without Him, is death.

It may be said, "Why all this? Why not go on like a brave man to meet your fate, careless of what that fate may be?"

"But what if this fate *should* depend on myself? Am I to be careless then?" I answer.

"The fate is so uncertain! If it be annihilation, why quail before it? Cowardice at least is contemptible."

"Is not indifference more contemptible? That one who has once thought should not care to go on to think? That this glory should perish — is it no grief? Is life not a good with all its pain? Ought one to be willing to part with a good? Ought he not to cling fast to it? Have you never grudged the coming sleep, because you must cease for the time to *be* so much as you were before?" For my part, I think the man who can go to sleep without faith in God has yet to learn what being is. He who knows not God cannot, however, have much to lose in losing being. And yet — and yet — did he never love man or woman or child? Is he content that there should be no more of it? Above all, is he content to go on with man and woman and child now, careless of whether the love is a perishable thing?

If it be, why does he not kill himself, seeing it is all a lie —

a false appearance of a thing too glorious to be fact, but for which our best nature calls aloud—and cannot have it? If one knew for certain that there was no life beyond this, then the noble thing would be to make the best of this, yea even then to try after such things as are written in the Gospel as we call it—for they *are* the noblest. That I am sure of, whatever I may doubt. But not to be sure of annihilation, and yet choose it to be true, and act as if it were true, seems to me to indicate a nature at strife with immortality—bound for the dust by its own choice—of the earth, and returning to the dust.

The man will say, "That is yielding everything. Let us eat and drink, for to-morrow we die. I am of the dust, for I believe in nothing beyond."

"No," I return. "I recognize another law in myself which seems to me infinitely higher. And I think that law is in you also, although you are at strife with it, and will revive in you to your blessed discontent. By that I will walk, and not by yours—a law which bids me strive after what I am not but may become—a law in me striving against the law of sin and down-dragging decay—a law which is one with my will, and, if true, must of all things make one at last. If I am made to live I ought not to be willing to cease."

This unwillingness to cease—above all, this unwillingness to cease to love my own, may be in me the sign, may *well* be in me the sign that I am made to live. Above all to pass away without the possibility of making reparation to those whom I have wronged, with no chance of saying *I am sorry—what shall I do for you? Grant me some means of delivering myself from this burden of wrong*—seems to me frightful. No God to help one to be good now! no God who cares whether one is good or not! if a God, then one who will not give His creature time enough to grow good, even if he is growing better, but will blot him out like a rain-drop! Great God, forbid—if thou art. If thou art not, then this, like all other prayers, goes echoing through the soulless vaults of a waste universe, from the thought of which its peoples recoil in horror. Death, then, is genial, soul-begetting, and love-creating; and Life is nowhere, save in the imaginations of the children of the grave. Whence, then, oh! whence came those their imaginations?

What better sign of immortality than the raising of the dead could God give? He cannot, however, be always raising the dead before our eyes; for then the holiness of death's ends would be a failure. We need death; only it shall be undone once and again for a time, that we may know it is not what it seems to us.

I have already said that probably we are not capable of being told in words what the other world is. But even the very report through the ages that the dead came back, as their friends had known them, with the old love unlost in the grave, with the same face to smile and bless, is precious indeed. That they remain the same in all that made them lovely, is the one priceless fact — if we may but hope in it as a fact. That we shall behold, and clasp, and love them again follows of simple necessity.

We cannot be sure of the report as if it were done before our own eyes, yet what a hope it gives even to him whose honesty and his faith together make him, like Martha, refrain speech, not daring to say *I believe* of all that is reported! I think such a one will one day be able to believe more than he even knows how to desire. For faith in Jesus will well make up for the lack of the sight of the miracle.

Does God, then, make death look what it is not? Why not let it appear what it is, and prevent us from forming false judgments of it?

It is our low faithlessness that makes us misjudge it, and nothing but faith could make us judge it aright. And that, while in faithlessness, we should thus misjudge it, is well. In what it appears to us, it is a type of what we are without God. But there is no falsehood in it. The dust must go back to the dust. He who believes in the body more than in the soul, cleaves to this aspect of death. He who believes in thought, in mind, in love, in truth, can see the other side — can rejoice over the bursting shell which allows the young oak to creep from its kernel-prison. The lower is true, but the higher overcomes and absorbs it.

"When the perfect comes, the imperfect will pass away." When the spirit of death is seen, the body of death vanishes from us. Death is God's angel of birth. We fear him. The dying stretches out loving hands of hope towards him. I do not believe that death is to the dying the dreadful thing it looks to the beholders. I think it is more like what the spirit may then be able to remember of its own birth as a child into this lower world, this porch of the heavenly. How will he love his mother then! and all humanity in her, and God who gave her, and God who gives her back!

The future lies dark before us, with an infinite hope in the darkness. To be at peace concerning it on any other ground than the love of God, would be an absolute loss. Better fear and hope and prayer, than knowledge and peace without the prayer.

To sum up: An express revelation in words would probably be little intelligible. In Christ we have an ever-growing revelation. He is the resurrection and the life. As we know Him we know our future.

In our ignorance lies a force of need, compelling us towards God.

In our ignorance likewise lies the room for the development of the simple will, as well as the necessity for arousing it. Hence this ignorance is but the shell of faith.

In this, as in all His miracles, our Lord *shows* in one instance what His Father is ever doing without showing it.

Even the report of this is the best news we can have from the *other* world — as we call it.

For Thought and Discussion

How important or necessary is a belief in the life beyond death to happiness now? to virtue? to a sense of well-being?

The Raising of the Widow's Son

1. What attitudes, and actions, should Christians cultivate towards death in order to bring their conduct into full harmony with their hope?

2. Why, do you think, does the Bible give so comparatively little description of the next life?

The Raising of the Daughter of Jairus

1. Why is it so precious to believe that God has "a heart like our own"? What Biblical statements and metaphors would encourage us to do so?

2. Why is a wonder "a poor thing for faith after all"?

3. What does Jesus mean by the words, "The child is not dead but sleeping"?

The Raising of Lazarus

1. What may be learned from the fact that Jesus never did a miracle for His own benefit?

2. Why was Jesus troubled in Mary's presence, and why did He weep?

3. What reasons may be given why the Bible records nothing of what Lazarus said —or experienced but may not have said —concerning his experience of the life beyond? Why do we "need death"?

NINE

THE GOVERNMENT OF NATURE

*T*he miracles I include in this class are the following:

1. The turning of water into wine, already treated of, given by St. John.

2. The draught of fishes, given by St. Luke.

3. The draught of fishes, given by St. John.

4. The feeding of the four thousand, given by St. Matthew and St. Mark.

5. The feeding of the five thousand, recorded by all the Evangelists.

6. The walking on the sea, given by St. Matthew, St. Mark, and St. John.

7. The stilling of the storm, given by St. Matthew, St. Mark, and St. Luke.

8. The fish bringing the piece of money, told by St. Matthew alone.

These miracles, in common with those already considered, have for their end the help or deliverance of man. They differ from those, however, in operating mediately, through a change upon external things, and not at once on their human subjects.

But besides the fact that they have to do with what we call nature, they would form a class on another ground. In those cases of disease, the miracles are for the setting right of what has gone wrong, the restoration of the order of things—namely, of the original condition of humanity. No doubt it is a law of nature that where there is sin there should be suffering; but even its cure helps to restore that righteousness which is highest nature. For the cure of suffering must not be confounded with the absence of suffering.

But the miracles of which I have now to speak, show themselves as interfering with what we may call the righteous laws of nature. Water should wet the foot, should engulf him who would tread its surface. Bread should come from the oven last, from the field first. Fishes should be now here, now there, according to laws ill understood of men. Wine should take ripening in the grape and in the bottle. In all these cases it is otherwise.

Yet even in these, I think, the restoration of an original law—the supremacy of righteous man, is foreshown. While a man cannot order his own house as he would, something is wrong in him, and therefore in his house. I think a true man should be able to rule winds and waters and loaves and fishes, for he comes of the Father who made the house for him. Had Jesus not been capable of these things, He might have been the best of men, but either He could not have been a perfect man, or the perfect God, if such there were, was not in harmony with the perfect man.

Man is not master in his own house because he is not

master in himself, because he is not a law unto himself—is not himself obedient to the law by which he exists. Harmony, that is law, alone is power. Discord is weakness. God alone is perfect, living, self-existent law.

I will try, in a few words, to give the ground on which I find it possible to accept these miracles. I cannot lay it down as for any other man. I do not wonder at most of those to whom the miracles are a stumbling-block. I do a little wonder at those who can believe in Christ and yet find them a stumbling-block.

How God creates, no man can tell. But as man is made in God's image, he may think about God's work, and dim analogies may arise out of the depth of his nature which have some resemblance to the way in which God works. I say then, that, as we are the offspring of God—the children of His will—like as the thoughts move in a man's mind, we live in God's mind. When God thinks anything, then that thing *is*. His thought of it is its life. Everything is because God thinks it into being. Can it then be very hard to believe that He should alter by a thought any form or appearance of things about us?

"It is inconsistent to work otherwise than by law."

True; but we know so little of this law that we cannot say what is essential in it, and what only the so far irregular consequence of the unnatural condition of those for whom it was made, but who have not yet willed God's harmony. We know so little of law that we cannot certainly say what would be an infringement of this or that law. That which at first sight appears as such, may be but the operating of a higher law which rightly dominates the other.

It is the law, as we call it, that a stone should fall to the ground. A man may place his hand beneath the stone, and then, *if his hand be strong enough,* it is the law that the stone shall not fall to the ground. The law has been lawfully prevented from working its full end. In similar ways, God might stop the working of one law by the intervention of another. Such intervention, if not understood by us, would be what we call a miracle. All I want to show here, is a conceivable region in which a miracle might take place without any violence done to the order of things. Let us beware lest what we call faith be but the mere assent of a mind which has cared and thought so little about the objects of its so-called faith, that it has never seen the difficulties they involve. Some such believers are the worst antagonists of true faith—the children of the Pharisees of old.

If any one say we ought to receive nothing of which we have no experience; I answer, there is in me a necessity, a desire before which all my experience shrivels into a mockery. Its complement must lie beyond. We ought, I grant, to accept nothing for which we cannot see the probability of some sufficient reason, but I thank God that this sufficient reason is not for me limited to the realm of experience. To suppose that it was would change the hope of a life that might be an ever-burning sacrifice of thanksgiving, into a poor struggle with events and things and chances—to doom the Psyche to perpetual imprisonment in the worm. I desire the higher; I care not to live for the lower. The one would make me despise my fellows and recoil with disgust from a self I cannot annihilate; the other fills me with humility, hope, and love. Is the preference for the one over the other foolish then—even to the meanest judgment?

A higher condition of harmony with law, may one day enable us to do things which must now *appear* an interruption of law. I believe it is in virtue of the absolute harmony in Him, His perfect righteousness, that God can create at all. If man were in harmony with this, if he too were righteous, he would inherit of his Father a something in his degree correspondent to the creative power in Him; and the world he inhabits, which is but an extension of his body, would, I think, be subject to him in a way surpassing his wildest dreams of dominion, for it would be the perfect dominion of holy law—a virtue flowing to and from him through the channel of a perfect obedience. I suspect that our Lord in all His dominion over nature, set forth only the complete man—man as God means him one day to be.

Why should He not know where the fishes were? or even make them come at His will? Why should not that will be potent as impulse in them? If we admit what I hail as the only fundamental idea upon which I can speculate harmoniously with facts, and as alone disclosing regions wherein contradictions are soluble, and doubts previsions of loftier truth—I mean the doctrine of the Incarnation—or if even we admit that Jesus was good beyond any other goodness we know, why should it not seem possible that the whole region of inferior things might be more subject to Him than to us? And if more, why not altogether? I believe that some of these miracles were the natural result of a physical nature perfect from the indwelling of a perfect soul, whose unity with the Life of all things and in all things was absolute—in a word, whose sonship was perfect.

If in the human form God thus visited His people, He would naturally show Himself Lord over their circumstances. He will not lord it over their minds, for such lordship is to Him abhorrent. They themselves must see and rejoice in acknowledging the lordship which makes them free. He revealed the Father as being *under* no law, but as law itself, and the cause of the laws we know—the cause of all harmony because Himself *the* harmony. Men had to be delivered not only from the fear of suffering and death, but from the fear, which is a kind of worship, of nature. Nature herself must be shown subject to the Father and to Him whom the Father had sent.

Men must believe in the great works of the Father through the little works of the Son. All that He showed was little to what God was doing. They had to be helped to see that it was God who did such things as often as they were done. He it is who causes the corn to grow for man. He gives every fish that a man eats. Even if things are terrible yet they are God's, and the Lord will still the storm for their faith in him—tame a storm, as a man might tame a wild beast—for His Father measures the waters in the hollow of His hand, and men are miserable not to know it. For Himself, I repeat, His faith is enough; He sleeps on His pillow, nor dreams of perishing.

On the individual miracles of this class, I have not much to say. The first of them was wrought in the animal kingdom.

The Draughts of Fishes (Luke 5:1-11; John 21:1-19)

He was teaching on the shore of the lake, and the people crowded Him. That He might speak with more freedom, He stepped into an empty boat, and having prayed Simon the owner of it, who was washing his nets near by, to thrust it a little from the shore, sat down, and no longer incommoded by the eagerness of His audience, taught them from the boat. When He had ended He told Simon to launch out into the deep, and let down his nets for a draught.

Simon had little hope of success, for there had been no fish there all night; but he obeyed, and caught such a multitude of fishes that the net broke. They had to call another boat to their aid, and both began to sink from the overload of fishes. But the great marvel of it wrought on the mind of Simon as every wonder tends to operate on the mind of an honest man: it brought his sinfulness before him. In self-abasement he fell down at Jesus' knees.

Whether he thought of any individual sins at the moment, we cannot tell; but he was painfully dissatisfied with himself. He knew he was not what he ought to be. I am unwilling however to believe that such a man desired, save, it may be, as a passing involuntary result of distress, to be rid of the holy presence. I judge rather that his feeling was like that of the centurion—that he felt himself unworthy to have the Lord in his boat. He may have feared that the Lord took him for a good man, and his honesty could not endure such a mistake: "Depart from me, for I am a sinful man, O Lord."

The Lord accepted the spirit, therefore *not* the word of his prayer.

"Do not be afraid; henceforth you will be catching men."

His sense of sinfulness, so far from driving the Lord from him, should draw other men to him. As soon as that cry broke from his lips, he had become fit to be a fisher of men. He had begun to abjure that which separated man from man.

After His resurrection, St. John tells us the Lord appeared one morning, on the shore of the lake, to some of His disciples, who had again been toiling all night in vain. He told them once more how to cast their net, and they were not able to draw it for the multitude of fishes.

"It is the Lord," said St. John, purer-hearted, perhaps therefore keener-eyed, than the rest.

Since the same thing had occurred before, Simon had become the fisher of men, but had sinned grievously against his Lord. He knew that Lord so much better now, however, that when he heard it was He, instead of crying *Depart from me,* he cast himself into the sea to go to Him.

The Feeding of the Thousands (Matthew 14:15-21; 15:32-39; Mark 6:30-44; 8:1-9; Luke 9:12-17; John 6:5-14)

I take next the feeding of the four thousand with the seven loaves and the few little fishes, and the feeding of the five thousand with the five loaves and the two fishes.

Concerning these miracles, I think I have already said almost all I have to say. If He was the Son of God, the bread might as well grow in His hands as the corn in the fields. It is, I repeat, only a doing in condensed form, hence one more easily associated with its real source, of that which God is for ever doing more widely, more slowly, and with more detail both of fundamental wonder and of circumstantial loveliness. Whence more fittingly might food come than from the hands of such an elder brother?

No doubt there will always be men who cannot believe it; happy are they who demand a good reason, and yet can believe a wonder! Associated with words which appeared to me foolish, untrue, or even poor in their content, I should not believe it. Associated with such things as He spoke, I can receive it with ease, and I cherish it with rejoicing.

It must be noted in respect of the feeding of the five thousand, that while the other evangelists merely relate the deed as done for the necessities of the multitude, St. John records also the use our Lord made of the miracle. It was the outcome of His essential relation to humanity. Of humanity He was ever the sustaining food. To humanity He was about to give Himself in an act of such utter devotion as could only by shadowed — now in the spoken, afterwards in the acted symbol of the eucharist.

The miracle was a type of His life as the life of the world, a sign that from Him flows all the weal of His creatures. The bread we eat is but its outer husk: the true bread is the Lord Himself, to have whom in us is eternal life. "Unless you eat the flesh of the Son of man and drink His blood you have no life in you." He knew that the grand figure would disclose to the meditation of the loving heart infinitely more of the truth of the matter than any possible amount of definition and explanation, and yet must ever remain far short of setting forth the holy fact to the boldest and humblest mind.

But lest they should start upon a wrong track for the interpretation of it, He says to His disciples afterwards, that this body of His should return to God; that what He had said concerning the eating of it had a spiritual sense: "It is the spirit that gives life; the flesh is of no avail" — for that. In words He contradicts what He said before, that they might see the words to have meant infinitely more than as words they were able to express. Not their bodies on His body, but their souls must live on His soul, by a union and communion of which the eating of His flesh and the drinking of His blood was, after all, but a poor and faint figure.

In this miracle, for the souls as for the bodies of men, He did and revealed the work of the Father. He who has once understood the meaning of Christ's words in connection with this miracle, can never be content they should be less than true concerning His Father in heaven. Whoever would have a perfect Father, must believe that He bestows His very being for the daily food of His creatures.

He who loves the glory of God will be very jealous of any word that would enhance His greatness by representing him incapable of suffering. Verily God has taken and will ever take and endure His share, His largest share of that suffering in and through which the whole creation groans for the sonship.

The Walking on the Sea (Matthew 14:22-33; Mark 6:45-52; John 6:16-21)

Follows at once the equally wonderful story of His walking on the sea to the help of His disciples. After the former miracle, the multitude would have taken Him by force to make Him their king. Any kind of honor they would readily give Him except that obedience for the truth's sake which was all He cared for.

He left them and went away into a mountain alone to pray to His Father. Likely He was weary in body, and also worn in spirit for lack of that finer sympathy which His disciples could not give Him, being very earthly yet. He who loves his fellows and labors among those who can ill understand him will best know what this weariness of our Lord must have been like. He had to endure the world-pressure of surrounding humanity in all its ungodlike phases. Hence even He, the everlasting Son of the Father, found it needful to retire for silence and room and comfort into solitary places.

There His senses would be free, and His soul could the better commune with the Father. There He gathered strength from the will of the Father for what yet remained to be done for the world's redemption. How little could the men below, who would have taken Him by force and made Him a king, understand of such communion! Yet every one of them must go hungering and thirsting and grasping in vain, until the door of that communion was opened for him. They would have made Him a king; He would make them poor in spirit, mighty in aspiration, all kings and priests unto God.

But amidst His prayer, He saw His disciples thwarted by a wind stronger than all their rowing. He descended the hill and walked forth on the water to their help.

If ignorant yet devout speculation may be borne with here, I venture to say that I think the change of some kind that was necessary somehow before the body of the Son of Man could, like the Spirit of old, move upon the face of the waters, passed, not upon the water, but, by the will of the Son of Man Himself, upon His own body. I shall have more to say concerning this in a following chapter. Now I merely add that we know nothing yet, or next to nothing, of the relation between a right soul and a healthy body. To some no doubt the notion of a healthy body implies chiefly a perfection of all the animal functions, which is, on the supposition, a matter of course. But what I should mean by an absolutely healthy body is, one entirely under the indwelling spirit, and responsive immediately to all the laws of its supremacy, whatever those laws may be in the divine ideal of a man.

As we are now, we find the diseased body tyrannizing over the almost helpless mind. The healthy body would be the absolutely obedient body. What power over His own dwelling a Savior coming fresh from the closest speech with Him who made that body for holy subjection, might have, who can tell! If I hear of any reasonable wonder resulting therefrom, I shall not find it hard to believe, and shall be willing to wait until I, pure, inhabit an obedient house, to understand the plain thing which is now a mystery. Meantime I can honor the laws I do know, and which honest men tell me they have discovered, no less than those honest men who think such as I foolish in employing the constructive faculty with regard to these things.

Nor would it be impossible to imagine how St. Peter might come within the sphere of the holy influence, so that he, too, for a moment should walk on the water. Faith will yet prove itself as mighty a power as it is represented by certain words of the Lord which are at present a stumbling-block even to devout Christians, who are able to accept them only by putting explanations upon them which render them unworthy of His utterance. When I say *a power,* I do not mean in itself, but as connecting the helpless with the helpful, as uniting the empty need with the full supply, as being the conduit through which it is right and possible for the power of the creating God to flow to the created necessity.

When the Lord got into the boat, the wind ceased, "and immediately," says St. John, "the boat was at the land to which they were going." As to whether the ceasing of the wind was by the ordinary laws of nature, or some higher law first setting such in operation, no one who has followed the spirit of my remarks will wonder that I do not care to inquire. They are all of one.

Nor, in regard to their finding themselves so quickly at the end of their voyage, will they wonder if I think that we may have just one instance of space itself being subject to the obedient God, and that His wearied disciples, having toiled and rowed hard for so long, might well find themselves at their desired haven as soon as they received Him into their boat. Either God is all in all, or He is nothing. Either Jesus is the Son of the Father, or He did no miracle. Either the miracles are fact, or I lost — not my faith in this man—but certain outward signs of truth which these very signs have aided me to discover and understand and see in themselves.

The miracle of the stilling of the storm naturally follows here.

The Stilling of the Storm (Matthew 8:23-27; Mark 4:35-41; Luke 8:22-25)

Why should not He, who taught His disciples that God numbered the very hairs of their heads, do what His Father is constantly doing—still storms—bring peace out of uproar? Of course, if the storm was stilled, it came about by natural causes—that is, by such as could still a storm. That anything should be done by unnatural causes—that is, cause not of the nature of the things concerned—is absurd. The sole question is whether Nature works alone, as some speculators think, or whether there is a soul in her, namely, an intent—whether these things are the result of thought, or whether they spring from a dead heart.

That things should go by a law which does not recognize the loftiest in him, a man feels to be a mockery of him. There lies little more satisfaction in such a condition of things than if the whole were the fortuitous result of ever conflicting, never combining forces. Wherever individual and various necessity, choice, and prayer, come in, there must be the present God, able and ready to fit circumstances to the varying need of the thinking, will-ing being He has created. Machinery will not do here—perfect as it may be.

That God might make a world to go on with absolute perfection to all eternity, I could easily believe; but where the gain?—nay, where the fitness, if He would train thinking beings to His own freedom? For such He must be ever present, ever have room to order things for their growth and change and discipline and enlightenment. The present living idea informing the cosmos is nobler than all forsaken perfection—nobler, as a living man is nobler than an automaton.

If one should say: "The laws of God ought to admit of no change," I answer: The same working of unalterable laws might under new circumstances *look* a breach of those laws. That God will never alter His laws, I fully admit and uphold, for they are the outcome of His truth and fact. But that He might not act in ways unrecognizable by us as consistent with those laws, I have yet to see reason ere I believe.

Why should His perfect will be limited by our understanding of that will? Should He be paralyzed because we are blind? That He should ever require us to believe of Him what we think wrong, I do not believe; that He should present to our vision what may be inconsistent with our half-digested and constantly changing theories, I can well believe. Why not—if only to keep us from petrifying an imperfect notion, and calling it an *Idea*?

What I would believe is, that a present God manages the direction of those laws, even as a man, in his inferior way, works out his own will in the midst and by means of those laws. Shall God create that which shall fetter and limit and enslave Himself? What should His laws, as known to us, be but the active mode in which He embodies certain truths —that mode also the outcome of His own nature? If so, they must be always capable of falling in with any, if not of effecting every, expression of His will.

The Money in the Fish's Mouth (Matthew 17:24-27)
There remains but one miracle of this class to consider—one to some minds involving greater difficulties than all the rest. They say the story of the fish with a piece of money in its mouth is more like one of the tales of eastern fiction than a sober narrative of the quiet-toned gospel. I acknowledge a likeness. Why might there not be some likeness between what God does and what man invents? But there is one noticeable difference. There is nothing of color in the style

of the story. No great roc, no valley of diamonds, no earthly grandeur whatever is hinted at in the poor bare tale.

Peter had to do with fishes every day of his life. An ordinary fish, taken with the hook, was here the servant of the Lord—and why should not the poor fish have its share in the service of the Master? What the scaly minister brought was no rich jewel, but a simple piece of money, just enough, I presume, to meet the demand of those whom, although they had no legal claim, our Lord would not offend by a refusal. For He never cared to stand upon His rights, or treat that as a principle which might be waived without loss of righteousness. I take for granted that there was no other way at hand for those poor men to supply the sum required of them.

For Thought and Discussion

1. Is it important to think about the nature of the miracles of Christ, or should they simply be accepted without further thought? Explain the statement: "Happy are they who demand a good reason, and yet can believe a wonder."

2. In MacDonald's view, how are the miracles treated in this chapter consistent with the workings of natural law? In the future, when redeemed men are glorified, what may their relation to nature be?

3. Discuss the implications of the following statements:
a. "Whoever would have a perfect Father, must believe that He bestows His very being for the daily food of His creatures." Discuss the ways in which God "bestows His very being" upon us.

b. "The present living idea informing the cosmos is nobler than all forsaken perfection—nobler, as a living man is nobler than an automaton." What is the role of the world, as it is, in training "thinking beings to His own freedom"?

TEN

MIRACLES OF DESTRUCTION

*I*f we regard the miracles of our Lord as an epitome of the works of His Father, there must be room for what we call destruction.

In the grand process of existence, destruction is one of the phases of creation; for the inferior must ever be giving way for the growth of the superior. The husk must crumble and decay that the seed may germinate and appear. As the whole creation passes on towards the sonship, death must ever be doing its sacred work about the lower regions, that life may ever arise triumphant, in its ascent towards the will of the Father.

The Withering of the Fig Tree (Matthew 21:18-22; Mark 11:12-14, 20-26)

I cannot therefore see good reason why the almost solitary

act of destruction recorded in the story should seem unlike
the Master. True, this kind is unlike the other class in this,
that it has only an all but solitary instance. He did not come
for the manifestation of such power. But why, when occasion appeared, should it not have its place? Why might not
the Lord, consistently with His help and His dealing, do
that in one instance which His Father is doing every day? It
is the indrawn sigh of the creating Breath.

Our Lord had already spoken the parable of the fig tree
that bore no fruit. This miracle was but the acted parable.
Here He puts into visible form that which before He had
embodied in words. All shapes of argument must be employed to arouse the slumbering will of men. Even the
obedience that comes of the lowest fear is a first step
towards an infinitely higher condition than that of the most
perfect nature created incapable of sin.

The right interpretation of the external circumstances,
however, is of course necessary to the truth of the miracle.
It seems to me to be the following. I do not know to whom I
am primarily indebted for it.

The time of the gathering of figs was near, but had not
yet arrived. Upon any fruitful tree one might hope to find a
few ripe figs, and more that were eatable. The Lord was
hungry as He went to Jerusalem from Bethany, and saw on
the way a tree with all the promise that a perfect foliage
could give. He went up to it, "to see if He could find anything on it." The leaves were all; fruit there was none in any
stage. The tree was a pretense. It fulfilled not that for which
it was sent.

Here was an opportunity in their very path of enforcing,
by a visible sign proceeding from Himself, one of the most
important truths He had striven to teach them. What He
had been saying was in Him a living truth. He condemned
the tree to become in appearance that which it was in fact —
a useless thing. When they passed the following morning, it
had withered away, was dried up from the roots.

He did not urge in words the lesson of the miracle-parable. He left that to work when the fate of fruitless Jerusalem should also have become fact. For the present the marvel of it possessed them too much for the reading of its lesson. Therefore, perhaps, our Lord makes little of the marvel and much of the power of faith, assuring them of answers to their prayers, but adding, according to St. Mark, that forgiveness of others is the indispensable condition of their own acceptance—fit lesson surely to hang on that withered tree.

The Repulsion of the Soldiers (John 18:1-6)

After all, the thing destroyed was only a tree. In respect of humanity there is but one distant approach to anything similar! In the pseudo-evangels there are several tales of vengeance—not one in these books. The fact to which I refer is recorded by St. John alone. It is, that when the "band of soldiers and some officers from the chief priests and the Pharisees" came to take Him, and "Jesus came forward and said to them, 'Whom do you seek?' " and in reply to theirs, had said, " 'I am He,' they drew back and fell to the ground."

There are one or two facts in connection with the record of this incident, which although not belonging quite immediately to my present design, I would yet note, with the questions they suggest.

The synoptical Gospels record the Judas-kiss: St. John does not.

St. John alone records the going backward and falling to the ground—prefacing the fact with the words, "Judas, who betrayed Him, was standing with them."

Had not the presence of Judas, then—perhaps his kiss— something to do with the discomfiture of these men? If so —and it seems to me probable—how comes it that St. John alone omits the kiss? St. John alone records the recoil. I repeat—if the kiss had to do with the recoil—as would seem from mystical considerations most probable, from artistic most suitable—why are they divided?

I think just because those who saw, saw each a part, and record only what they saw or had testimony concerning. Had St. John seen the kiss, he who was so capable of understanding the mystical fitness of the connection of such a kiss with such a recoil, could hardly have omitted it, especially seeing he makes such a point of the presence of Judas. Had he been an inventor, here is just such a thing as he would have invented; and just here his record is barer than that of the rest—bare of the one incident which would have best helped out his own idea of the story. The consideration is suggestive.

But why this exercise of at least repellent (which is half-destructive) force, reminding us of Milton's words—

Yet half his strength he put not forth, but checked
His thunder in mid volley?

It may have had to do with the repentance of Judas which followed. It may have had to do with the future history of the Jewish men who composed that band. But I suspect the more immediate object of our Lord was the safety of His disciples. As soon as the men who had gone backward and fallen to the ground, had risen and again advanced, He repeated the question—"Whom do you seek?" "Jesus of Nazareth," they replied. "I told you that I am He," said the Lord again, but added, now that they had felt His power, "If you seek me, let these men go." St. John's reference in respect of these words to a former saying of the Lord, strengthens this conclusion.

And there was no attempt even to lay hands on them. He had astonished and terrified His captors to gain of them His sole request—that His friends should go unhurt. There was work for them to do in the world; and He knew besides that they were not yet capable of enduring for His sake.

At all events it was neither for vengeance nor for self-preservation that this gentlest form of destruction was manifested. I suspect it was but another shape of the virtue that went forth to heal. A few men fell to the ground that His disciples might have time to grow apostles, and redeem the world with the news of Him and His Father. For the sake of humanity the fig-tree withered; for the resurrection of the world, His captors fell. Small hurt and mighty healing.

Daring to interpret the work of the Father from the work of the Son, I would humbly believe that all destruction is for creation—that, even for this, death alone is absolutely destroyed. [Death now destroys that which] stands in the way of the outgoing of the Father's will, [and will itself be destroyed] when men are made holy.

God does destroy; but not life. Its outer forms yield that it may grow, and growing pass into higher embodiments, in which it can grow yet more. That alone will be destroyed which has the law of death in itself—namely, sin. Sin is death, and death must be swallowed up of hell. Life, that is God, is the heart of things, and destruction must be destroyed. For this victory endless *forms* of life must yield—even the *form* of the life of the Son of God Himself must yield upon the cross, that the life might arise a life-giving spirit.

His own words must be fulfilled—"If I do not go away, the Counselor will not come to you." All spirit must rise victorious over form; and the form must die lest it harden to stone around the growing life. No form is or can be great enough to contain the truth which is its soul; for all truth is infinite, being a thought of God. It is only in virtue of the flowing away of the form, that is death, and the ever gathering of new form behind, that is birth or embodiment, that any true revelation is possible.

On what other terms shall the infinite embrace the finite but the terms of an endless change, an enduring growth, a recognition of the divine as for ever above and beyond, a forgetting of that which is behind, a reaching unto that which is before? Therefore destruction itself is holy. It is as if the Eternal said, "I will show myself; but think not to hold me in any form in which I come. The form is not I." The still small voice is ever reminding us that the Lord is neither in the earthquake nor the wind nor the fire, but in the lowly heart that finds Him everywhere. The material can cope with the eternal only in virtue of everlasting evanescence.

For Thought and Discussion
What part does destruction have in the creative process? How may it be said to be "holy"?

The Withering of the Fig Tree:
1. Precisely what is the truth this incident teaches?

2. How are the precepts of Mark 11:22-26 related to the lesson the dead fig tree illustrates?

The Repulsion of the Soldiers
For what reasons did Jesus perform this act? What may this incident possibly have to do with the presence of Judas?

ELEVEN

THE
RESURRECTION

*T*he works of the Lord He Him-
self represents as given Him of the Father. It matters little
whether we speak of His resurrection as a miracle wrought
by Himself, or wrought in Him by the Father. If He was one
with the Father, the question cannot be argued, seeing that
Jesus apart from the Father is not a conceivable idea. It is
only natural that He who had power to call from the grave
the body which had lain there for four days, should have
power over the body He had Himself laid down, to take it
again with reanimating possession.

For distinctly do I hold that He took again the same body
in which He had walked about on the earth, suffered, and
yielded unto death. In the same body — not merely the same
form, in which He had taught them, He appeared again to

His disciples, to give them the final consolations of a visible presence, before departing for the sake of yet higher presence in the spirit of truth, a presence no longer limited by even the highest forms of the truth.

It is not surprising that the records of such a marvel, grounded upon the testimony of men and women bewildered first with grief, and next all but distracted with the sudden inburst of a gladness too great for that equanimity which is indispensable to perfect observation, should not altogether correspond in the minutiae of detail. All knew that the Lord had risen indeed. What matter whether some of them saw one or two angels in the tomb? The first who came saw one angel inside the sepulchre. One at a different time saw two inside. What wonder then that one of the records should say of them all, that they saw two angels?

I do not care to set myself to the reconciliation of the differing reports. Their trifling disagreement is to me even valuable from its truth to our human nature. All I care to do is to suggest to any one anxious to understand the records the following arrangement of facts.

When Mary Magdalene found the tomb empty, not seeing, or heedless of the angel, she forsook her companions, and ran to the chief of the disciples to share the agony of this final loss. Perhaps something might yet be done to rescue the precious form, and lay it aside with all futile honors. With Peter and John she returned to the grave, whence, in the mean time, her former companions, having seen and conversed with the angel inside, had departed to find their friends. Peter and John, having, the one entered, the other looked into the tomb, and seen only the folded garments of desertion, returned home, but Mary lingered weeping by the place which was not now even the grave of the beloved, so utterly had not only He but the signs of Him vanished.

As she wept, she stooped down into the sepulchre. There

sat the angels in holy contemplation, one at the head, the other at the feet where the body of Jesus had lain. Peter nor John had beheld them. To the eyes of Mary as of the other women, they were manifest. It is a lovely story that follows, full of marvel, as how should it not be?

St. John's Account (John 20)
"Woman, why are you weeping?" said the angels.

"Because they have taken away my Lord, and I do not know where they have laid Him," answered Mary, and turning away, tear-blinded, saw the gardener, as she thought.

'Woman, why are you weeping?" repeats the gardener. "Whom do you seek?"

Hopelessness had dulled every sense: not even a start at the sound of His voice!

"Sir, if you have carried Him away, tell me where you have laid Him, and I will take Him away."

"Mary!"

"Rabboni!"

"Do not hold me; for I have not yet ascended to the Father; but go to my brethren, and say to them, I am ascending to my Father and your Father, to my God and your God."

She had the first sight of Him. It would almost seem that, arrested by her misery, He had delayed His ascent, and shown Himself sooner than His first intent. "Do not hold me, for I have not yet ascended." She was about to grasp Him with the eager hands of reverent love. Why did he refuse the touch?

Doubtless the tone of the words deprived them of any sting. Doubtless the self-respect of the woman was in no way wounded by the master's recoil. For the rest, we know so little of the new conditions of His bodily nature, that nothing is ours beyond conjecture. It may be, for anything I know, that there were even physical reasons why she should not yet touch Him. But my impression is that, after the hard work accomplished, and the form in which He had wrought and suffered resumed, He must have the Father's embrace first, as after a long absence any man would seek first the arms of his dearest friend.

It may well be objected to this notion, that He had never been absent from God—that in His heart He was at home with Him continually. And yet the body with all its limitations, with all its partition-walls of separation, is God's, and there must be some way in which even *it* can come into a willed relation with Him to whom it is nearer even than to ourselves, for it is the offspring of His will, or—as the prophets of old would say—the work of His hands.

That which God has invented and made, which has its very origin in the depth of His thought, *can* surely come nigh to God. Therefore I think that in some way which we cannot understand, Jesus would now seek the presence of the Father; would, having done the work which He had given Him to do, desire first of all to return in the body to Him who had *sent* Him by giving Him a body. Hence although He might delay His return at the sound of the woman's grief, He would rather *she* did not touch Him first.

If any one thinks this founded on too human a notion of the Savior, I would only reply that I suspect a great part of our irreligion springs from our disbelief in the humanity of God. There lie endless undiscovered treasures of grace. After He had once ascended to the Father, He not only appeared to His disciples again and again, but their hands handled the word of life, and He ate in their presence. He had been to His Father, and had returned that they might know Him lifted above the grave and all that region in which death has power.

For in regard of this glorified body of Jesus, we must note that it appeared and disappeared at the will of its owner. It would seem also that other matter yielded and gave it way. Even space itself was in some degree subjected to it. Upon

the first of these, the record is clear. If any man say he cannot believe it, my only answer is that I can. If he ask how it
could be, the nearest I can approach to an answer is to indicate the region in which it may be possible: the border-land
where thought and matter meet is the region where all
marvels and miracles are generated.

The wisdom of this world can believe that matter generates mind. What seems to me the wisdom from above can
believe that mind generates matter—that matter is but the
manifest mind. On this supposition matter may well be
subject to mind; much more, if Jesus be the Son of God, His
own body must be subject to His will. I doubt, indeed, if the
condition of any man is perfect before the body he inhabits
is altogether obedient to his will—before, through his own
absolute obedience to the Father, the realm of his own rule
is put under him perfectly.

It may be objected that although this might be credible
of the glorified body of even the human resurrection, it is
hard to believe that the body which suffered and died on
the cross could become thus plastic to the will of the indwelling spirit. But I do not see why that which was born of
the spirit of the Father, should not be so interpenetrated
and possessed by the spirit of the Son, that, without the loss
of one of its former faculties, it should be endowed with
many added gifts of obedience.

Why was this miracle needful?

Perhaps, for one thing, that men should not limit Him, or
themselves in Him, to the known forms of humanity. For
another, that the best hope might be given them of a life
beyond the grave; that their instinctive desires in that direction might thus be infinitely developed and assured. I suspect, however, that it followed just as the natural consequence of all that preceded.

If Christ be risen, then is the grave of humanity itself
empty. We have risen with Him, and death has henceforth
no dominion over us. Of every dead man and woman it may

be said: He—she—is not here, but is risen and gone before us. Ever since the Lord lay down in the tomb, and behold it was but a couch whence He arose refreshed, we may say of every brother: He is not dead, but he sleeps. He too is alive and shall arise from his sleep.

The way to the tomb may be hard, as it was for Him; but we who look on, see the hardness and not the help. We see the suffering but not the sustaining: that is known only to the dying and to God. They can tell us little of this, and nothing of the glad safety beyond.

With any theory of the conditions of our resurrection, I have scarcely here to do. It is to me a matter of positively no interest whether or not, in any sense, the matter of our bodies shall be raised from the earth. It is enough that we shall possess forms capable of revealing ourselves and of bringing us into contact with God's other works. They shall be forms in which the idea, so blurred and broken in these, shall be carried out. They will remain so like the former, that friends shall doubt not a moment of the identity, but they shall come so unlike, that the tears of recognition shall be all for the joy of the gain and the gratitude of the loss.

Not to believe in mutual recognition beyond, seems to me a far more reprehensible belief than that in the resurrection itself. I can well understand how a man should not believe in any life after death. I will confess that although probabilities are for it, *appearances* are against it. But that a man, still more a woman, should believe in the resurrection of the very same body of Jesus, who took pains that His friends should recognize Him therein, and yet not believe that friend shall embrace friend in the mansions prepared for them, is to me astounding.

Such a shadowy resumption of life I should count unworthy of the name of resurrection. Then indeed would the grave be victorious, not alone over the body, not alone over all which made the life of this world precious and by which we arose towards the divine—but also victorious over the soul. Henceforth it should be blind and deaf to what in virtue of loveliest memories would have added a new song to the praises of the Father, a new glow to the love that had wanted but that to make it perfect. In truth I am ashamed of even combating such an essential falsehood.

What seemed to the disciples the final acme of disappointment and grief, the vanishing of His body itself, was in reality the first sign of the dawn of an illimitable joy. He was not there because He had risen.

For Thought and Discussion

1. MacDonald insists here, and elsewhere, that "Jesus apart from the Father is not a conceivable idea." In the sermon "Life," he writes: "The worst heresy, next to that of dividing religion and righteousness, is to divide the Father from the Son —in thought or feeling or action or intent; to represent the Son as doing that which the Father does not Himself do" (Creation in Christ, p. 192). *Why is this truth of such crucial importance?*

2. What are the implications of the statement: " . . . I suspect a great part of our irreligion springs from our disbelief in the humanity of God. There lie endless undiscovered treasures of grace"?

TWELVE

THE TRANSFIGURATION

(Matthew 17:1-9; Mark 9:1-9; Luke 9:28-36)

I have judged it fitting to close this series of meditations with some thoughts on the Transfiguration, believing the story to be as it were a window through which we gain a momentary glimpse of the region whence all miracles appear—a glimpse vague and dark for all the transfiguring light, for God Himself is "by abundant clarity invisible." In the story we find a marvellous change, a lovely miracle, pass upon the form itself whence the miracles flowed, as if the pent-up grace wrought mightily upon the earthen vessel which contained it.

Our Lord would seem to have repeatedly sought some hill at eventide for the solitude such a place alone could afford Him. It must often have been impossible for Him to find any other chamber in which to hold communion with

His Father undisturbed. This, I think, was one of such occasions. He took with Him the favored three, whom also He took apart from the rest in the garden of Gethsemane, to retire even from them a little, that He might be alone with the Father, yet know that His brothers were near Him. The ocean of human need was thus drawn upwards in an apex of perfect prayer towards the throne of the Father.

I think this, His one only material show, if we except the entry into Jerusalem upon the ass, took place in the night. Then the son of Joseph the carpenter was crowned, not His head only with a crown placed thereon from without, but His whole person a crown of light born in Him and passing out from Him. According to St. Luke He went up to the mountain to pray; "now Peter and those who were with Him were *heavy with sleep.*" St. Luke also says that "on the next day, when they had come down from the mountain," that miracle was performed which St. Matthew and St. Mark represent as done *immediately* on the descent. From this it appears more than likely that the night was spent upon the mountain.

St. Luke says that "the appearance of His countenance was altered, and His raiment became dazzling white." St. Matthew says, "His face shone like the sun, and His garments became white as light." St. Mark says, "His garments became glistening, intensely white, as no fuller on earth could bleach them." St. Luke is alone in telling us that it was while He prayed that this change passed upon Him. He became outwardly glorious from inward communion with His Father.

But we shall not attain to the might of the meaning, if we do not see what was the more immediate subject of His prayer. It is, I think, indicated in the fact, also recorded by St. Luke, that the talk of His heavenly visitors was "of His departure, which He was to accomplish at Jerusalem." Associate with this fact that His talk with His disciples, as they came down the mountain, pointed in the same direc-

tion, and that all open report of the vision was to be with-
held until He should have risen from the dead, and it will
appear most likely that the Master, oppressed with the
thought of that which now drew very nigh, sought the comfort and sympathy of His Father, praying in the prospect of
His decease.

Let us observe then how, in heaving off the weight of this
awful shadow by prayer, He did not grow calm and re-
signed alone, if He were ever other than such, but His faith
broke forth so triumphant over the fear, that it shone from
Him in physical light. Every cloud of sorrow or dread,
touched with such a power of illumination, is itself changed
into a glory. The radiance goes hand in hand with the
coming decay and the three days' victory of death. It is as a
foretaste of His resurrection, a putting on of His new glorified body for a moment while He was yet in the old body
and the awful shadow yet between.

It may be to something like this as taking place in other
men that the apostle refers when he says: "We shall not all
sleep, but we shall all be changed." That coming death was
to be but as the overshadowing cloud, from which the glory
should break anew and for ever. The transfiguration then
was the divine defiance of the coming darkness.

Let us now speculate for a moment upon the relation of
the spiritual and physical manifested in it. He became, I
repeat, outwardly glorious from inward communion with
His Father. In like circumstance, the face of Moses shone
marvellously. And what wonder? What should make a
man's face shine, if not the presence of the Holy? if not
communion with the Father of his spirit? In the transfiguration of Jesus we have, I think, just the perfect outcome
of those natural results of which we have the first signs in
Moses—the full daylight, of which his shining face was as
the dawn. Thus, like the other miracles, I regard it as simply
a rare manifestation of the perfect working of nature.

Who knows not that in moments of lofty emotion, in

which self is for the time forgotten, the eyes shine, and the face is so transfigured that we are doubtful whether it be not in a degree absolutely luminous! I say once more, in the Lord we find the perfecting of all the dull hints of precious things which common humanity affords us. If so, what a glory must await every lowliest believer, since the communion of our elder brother with His Father and our Father, a communion for whose perfecting in us He came, caused not only His face to shine, but the dull garments He wore to become white as snow through the potency of the permeating light issuing from His whole person!

The outer man shone with the delight of the inner man — for His Father was with Him — so that even His garments shared in the glory. Such is what the presence of the Father will do for every man. May I not add that the shining of the garments is a type of the glorification of everything human when brought into its true relations by and with the present God?

Keeping the same point of view, I turn now to the resurrection with which the whole fact is so closely associated. I think the virtue of divine presence which thus broke in light from the body of Jesus is the same by which His risen body, half molten in power, was rendered plastic to the will of the indwelling spirit. What if this light were the healing agent of the bodies of men, as the deeper other light from which it sprung is the healing agent of themselves? Are not the most powerful of the rays of light invisible to our vision?

Some will object that this is a too material view of life and its facts. I answer that the question is whether I use the material to interpret the spiritual, as I think I do, or to account for it, as I know I do not. In my theory, the spiritual *both* explains and accounts for the material.

If the notions we have of what we may call *material light* render it the only fitting image to express the invisible Truth, the being of God, there must be some closest tie between them — not of connection only, but of unity. Such a fitness could not exist without such connection. The essential truth of God it must be that creates its own visual image in the sun that enlightens the world.

When man who is the image of God is filled with the presence of the eternal, he too, in virtue of his divine nature thus for the moment ripened to glory, radiates light from his very person. Where, when, or how the inner spiritual light passes into or generates outward physical light, who can tell? This border-land, this touching of what we call mind and matter, is the region of miracles—of material creation, I might have said, which is *the* great—I suspect, the *only* miracle. But if matter be the outcome of spirit, and body and soul be one man, then, if the soul be radiant of truth, what can the body do but shine?

I conjecture then, that truth, which is light in the soul, might not only cast out disease, which is darkness in the body, but change that body even without the intervention of death, into the likeness of the body of Jesus, capable of all that could be demanded of it. Except by violence I do not think the body of Jesus could have died. No physiologist can tell why man should die. I think a perfect soul would be capable of keeping its body alive. An imperfect one cannot fill it with light in every part—cannot thoroughly inform the brute matter with life.

The transfiguration of Jesus was but the visible outbreak of a life so strong as to be life-giving, life-restoring. The flesh it could melt away and evermore renew. Such a body might well walk upon the stormiest waters. A body thus responsive to and interpenetrative of light, which is the visible life, could have no sentence of death in it. It would never have died.

But I find myself in regions where I dare tread no further for the darkness of ignorance. I see many glimmers: they are too formless and uncertain.

When or how the light died away, we are not told. My own fancy is that it went on shining but paling all the night upon the lonely mount, to vanish in the dawn of the new day. When He came down from the mountain the virtue that dwelt in Him went forth no more in light to the eyes, but in healing to the poor torn frame of the epileptic boy. So He vanished at last from the eyes of His friends, only to draw nearer—with a more intense and healing presence—to their hearts and minds.

Even so come, Lord Jesus.

For Thought and Discussion

1. What to MacDonald's mind is the significance of the Transfiguration? What is its relation to the truth that "God is light, and in Him is no darkness at all"?

2. How is the Transfiguration related to Christ's approaching death? to His resurrection?

3. Explain the statement that, like the other miracles, this one also is "simply a rare manifestation of the perfect working of nature."

INDEX OF MIRACLES

INDEX OF SCRIPTURE PASSAGES

INDEX OF TOPICS